Engendering Citizenship in Egypt

LEILA FAWAZ, GENERAL EDITOR

The History and Society of the Modern Middle East

LEILA FAWAZ, GENERAL EDITOR

Within the Circle: Parents and Children in an Arab Village

ANDREA B. RUGH

Engendering Citizenship in Egypt

THE HISTORY AND SOCIETY OF THE
MODERN MIDDLE EAST

SELMA BOTMAN

COLUMBIA UNIVERSITY PRESS I NEW YORK

Columbia University Press
Publishers Since 1893
New York   Chichester, West Sussex
Copyright © 1999 Columbia University Press
All rights reserved

Library of Congress Cataloging-in-Publication Data
Botman, Selma.
    Engendering Citizenship in Egypt / Selma Botman.
        p.   cm. — (History and society of the modern Middle East)
    Includes bibliographical references (p.   ) and index.
    ISBN 978-0-231-11299-4 (pbk. : alk. paper)
        1. Women in politics—Egypt—History—20th century. 2. Political
    culture—Egypt—History—20th century. 3. Women—Egypt—Social
    conditions. 4. Egypt—Politics and government—1919–1952.
    5. Egypt—Politics and government—1952–   I. Title. II. Series:
    History and society of the modern Middle East series.
    HQ1236.5.E3B68   1998
    305.42'0962—dc21
                                                          98-36348
                                                          CIP

Casebound editions of Columbia University Press books are
printed on permanent and durable acid-free paper.

Printed in the United States of America

for Erica and Megan

CONTENTS

Preface   ix

CHAPTER 1 | Engendering Citizenship   I
CHAPTER 2 | Liberalism, Nationalism, and Gender   18
CHAPTER 3 | Women and the State During the
              Nasir Years   50
CHAPTER 4 | Gender Asymmetry During the Regimes
              of Anwar Sadat and Husni Mubarak   75
CHAPTER 5 | Middle Eastern Patriarchy   107

Notes   117
Selected Bibliography   125
Index   139

PREFACE

THIS STUDY EXPLORES THE EXPERIENCE of citizenship for Egyptian women in three distinct political periods of the twentieth century. It describes Egyptian political culture and reveals how women have at times inserted themselves into public life and how they have also been excluded, by political, religious, and cultural forces, from civic activity and full participation in civil society. Accepting that the politics of gender are neither accidental nor a fact of nature, the work asserts that gender hierarchies have been created both in the family and in society and have resulted in inequality in politics, the workplace, and social life.[1] Women's subordination in Egypt can be traced, in different ways, to religious law and custom, limited participation in the formal workforce, rapid population growth, and a legacy of precapitalist ideology.[2] Borrowing social scientist Amal Rassam's paradigm, this work considers the social organization of power, the ideological and institutional means of controlling women's sexuality, and the sexual division of labor,[3] highlighting the complexity and interdependence of men's and women's activities. It provides insight into the nature of political organization, the sources of power, and the implications of hierarchical domination.

While social roles in Egypt have been difficult to change, change has come to the family and to society, especially in the last fifty years, not because of an ideological revolution or through political necessity but because material forces have altered people's lives. The migration of men in search of employment, the weakening of extended family relations, increasing urbanization, improved education, and economic necessity have driven women into the workplace, adding complexity to life and leading to some reorganization of gender relations. Typically, social transformation is fraught with conflict and dislocation and Egypt is no exception: tracking these shifts forms a central component of this book.

The Egyptian family is given an important focus of attention because it is here that the areas of politics, economics, religion, and social life intersect. In the family men and women act out the roles they have learned as children and teach those roles to the next generation. Egyptian men are the decision makers and the undisputed heads of household; women are legal and social dependents whose productive and reproductive activities are regarded as comparatively insignificant. Gender relations in the family are mirrored in other parts of society even though developments in education, job training, and political organization have widened opportunities for women. Moreover, because family relations are governed by Sharia law, the religious traditions that enforce gender inequality are considered in this book.

Linking women almost exclusively to the home and family and centering social conformity in women's so-called natural inclinations are practices not confined to Egypt. They are to be found in societies around the world. In a host of countries women share the common experience of being outside the mainstream of economic and political power because their primary identity is that of wife and mother. Hester Eisenstein's assertion that the association of women with the private sphere and men with the public sphere has hardened over time into a truism and an ideology has particular application to Egypt.[4] While social changes take place, men are still connected to work, politics, and religion in its institutional forms, remain at the center of intellectual and cultural life, and continue to exercise power and authority. Women are associated with home, family, children, domestic life, and sexuality. Within these carefully constructed spheres women are confined, controlled, and sometimes concealed.

In Egypt women's relationship to the power structure has largely been framed by men who have sought to preserve patriarchal conditions of dominance. The asymmetrical construction of social relations in both the public arena and in the family have weakened women's repeated efforts to alter existing circumstances. Granted only a marginal role in the social contract, women's relationship to civil society has been tenuous. Throughout modern Egyptian political history men's dominance over women has restricted women's freedom and blocked their access to formal power.

During the age of liberal democracy in Egypt from 1923 to 1952 political, social, and economic life evolved and relations between men and women reflected a combination of postharem family life and nationalist activity by people of all social classes and both genders. These decades were transitional, representing partial Egyptian independence from British rule. Cultural authenticity and nationalism dominated the public discourse, remaining in force even after the monarchy was overthrown by nationalist military officers in 1952. The liberalization of women's public participation in the areas of education, employment, and voluntary social service compared to the unreformed control men maintained in the private domain of the family. Upper-class women accepted the patriarchal character of the Muslim family in exchange for new rights in the public arena.[5] In the liberal era women's citizenship excluded female suffrage and focused on the acceptance of cultural nationalism as a patriotic imperative in light of Egypt's ongoing struggle for national independence.

In the following period Nasirism was constructed around the themes of nationalism, secularism, state-dominated ideological control, and a centrally planned economy. Citizenship allowed women the vote, access to public office, and increased visibility in society. Women formed new gender identities directly linked to the social and political changes accomplished during the Nasir regime and believed that their contributions to the new republic were indispensable. Although women made impressive public gains, most notably through formal paid employment and considerably expanded educational opportunity, family relations changed little. Women continued to be responsible for traditional domestic tasks and the customary hierarchy of family life went unchallenged.

During the phase from 1970 to the present there has been a shift away from Nasir's radicalism to a more socially conservative but economically liberal philosophy. Islamic fundamentalism is on the rise and is characterized by militant anti-Western nationalism and indigenous cultural, religious, and historical traditions. Islam competes with secularism but has produced a groundswell of support for local cultural authenticity in opposition to the culture of the West. Gender asymmetry continues, and perhaps increases, despite concerted feminist efforts to alter the patriarchal nature of family and public life. Citizenship for women is consistently challenged by fundamentalists who believe women's place is exclusively in the home. Identity becomes increasingly complex for women since economic necessity requires that they work for wages while society's dominant values encourage them to return to the family.

This book submits that a rearticulation of gender relations in Egypt will succeed only if connected to a movement for democratization in the family and in the state. This will be a formidable task. Democrats and feminists who articulate a forward-looking and secular doctrine continue to be challenged by Egypt's history of state-centered control over political and social activities and by the strength of the fundamentalist movement in the country.

This work was conceived both as a contribution to the corpus of material on the political history of Egypt and to the growing literature on gender in developing societies. It is not designed to be a positivist account of women's activities in Egypt or an empirical record of what women did at any particular time. Rather, it presents comparative information about women at various points in Egypt's political development and addresses the question, How is citizenship defined in Egypt and by whom?

A number of people provided encouragement and helped facilitate the publication of this book. Ann Tickner acted as both a soulmate and an inspiration not only during our years as colleagues at College of the Holy Cross but since that time as well. Leila Fawaz and Feroz Ahmed read the manuscript and made valuable suggestions. Special thanks to my husband, Tom Birmingham, who patiently reviewed the book in various forms, shared his considerable wisdom, and made constructive recommendations. As always, I am the beneficiary of his many talents, his intellect, and his consistent support. Erica and Megan provided me with the perspective that only children can offer and continually reassure me that the future holds promise.

I would like to thank the National Endowment for the Humanities and the College of the Holy Cross for advancing my research through grants and fellowships, acknowledge the Center for Middle Eastern Studies at Harvard for allowing me access to the university's libraries, and extend appreciation to William M. Bulger, president of the University of Massachusetts, for support of this project.

Engendering Citizenship in Egypt

CHAPTER ONE | Engendering Citizenship

USING GENDER AS AN EPISTEMOLOGY to explain what we know about social relations and how we know it, this study seeks to clarify how the category of citizenship for women in Egypt has been created and recreated in three distinct periods—the nationalist and semiliberal constitutional phase from the early 1920s through World War II, the state-run socialist regime of Abd al-Nasir, and the open door (*infitah*) years from the 1970s through the 1990s. This work also seeks to explain how women's status affected their participation in political, cultural, and social life in those times. It charts the efforts of women to change or sometimes accommodate the social, political, and legal conditions in the country and traces their public rights, cultural restrictions, and struggles in civil society. Incorporating gender into politics and citizenship presupposes the notion that men and women deserve to be viewed as political and social equals.

By examining the interrelationships of women and men in the context of Egypt's evolving socioeconomic and political system, we discover that the knowledge generated by experience is socially constructed,[1] that is, made up of a set of ideas, symbols, and events conceived by both groups interactively. To determine whether that knowledge is employed for the purpose of domination and control or whether it can be altered to eliminate that domination, it is first important to understand in what ways Egyptian women have acknowledged their own subordination and acquiesced in it, how and in what circumstances they have resisted dependence, and what results have been achieved. Beyond that, we should consider whether there are models Egyptian women can adopt in their attempt to alter the political and social circumstances in which they live.

This work questions how gender-based hierarchies have been formed in Egypt and how they have been ideologically legitimated and socially maintained. It attempts to account for the difficulties women face trying to break into the traditional power structure and the formal economic system and examines women's efforts to effect structural change in a society in which gender asymmetry in laws, traditions, and even identities has transcended generations, social classes, and places of residence. By looking at how women's self-identities have changed over time in different ideological and economic periods as well as how men's views of women can be transformed through state intervention or religious intercession, our understanding of the complexities of gender roles deepens.

Women as Citizens, Mothers, and Historical Characters

In Egypt, as in other societies, gender, class, religious experience, and the particular political system in existence at a given time combine to define the status of men and women. Egyptian women are separated by social class but in general share a common subordination to men. Some observers of the country's social relations attribute the unequal status of men and women to biological characteristics and especially to the fact that women bear children. Others suggest that men exploit the "nature" argument in order to reinforce their own preeminence in domestic and societal matters. In both cases public life is separated from private life for Egyptian women with tangible consequences. Perceived as naturally belonging to the private world of the family, where freedom and equality do not prevail and where rights and responsibilities are narrowly defined, women have not been granted equal citizenship rights and have not been included in civil society in ways parallel to men.

For decades the topic of citizenship received considerable attention from social and political scientists. The renowned sociologist T. H. Marshall, the more contemporary theorists Stuart Hall and David Held, and others have posited that basic human equality is an essential requirement for full membership in a community.[2] They have argued that citizenship presupposes equality of rights, responsibilities, and opportunities and produces in individuals the feelings of inclusion and loyalty. The citizen participates in the public life of the community, enjoys political rights, contributes to its social and economic strength, and obtains entitlements in return.[3] Yet, in keeping with the lack of attention paid to women in political society, conventional studies of citizenship have overlooked the significance of gender and have concentrated instead on supposedly gender-neutral civil, political, and social rights. This work, in contrast, presents a more complete account of Egyptian civil society by incorporating gender into politics and citizenship.

The effect of omitting women from studies of citizenship and their rare appearance in mainstream studies of Egypt tend to skew our understanding of the country's history and politics. This void effectively marginalizes half the population, implicitly rendering powerless and unimportant women's activities in the home, the workplace, the community, and the public arena at large. When studies exclude women it is easy to conclude that they have been both figuratively and literally secluded in harems and hidden behind veils. By studying Egyptian politics and society through a gender lens, women become participants in real life, and women and men are seen to be constantly interacting to create or alter the conditions in which they live and work.

While in the past it had been customary and entirely conventional to study the political, economic, and religious beliefs and movements of the politically active, that is, of men, studying women had been much more controversial. Indeed, when surveying the standard texts and respected monographs written about Egypt, one finds that the subject of gender had been largely disregarded until very recently and that the contributions of women to the economy, community, family, and politics ignored. The way women fit into civil society was not considered by many political theorists who simply separated society into public (economic and political) and private (domestic, familial, and intimate) domains.

Recently feminist scholars of Middle Eastern and Western societies have challenged this public/private dichotomy and argued that the two realms are inherently interconnected and interdependent. Rejecting the tendency toward compartmentalization, they have insisted instead that men's domination over women in politics is grounded in and reflected by the power men hold over women in the family. They acknowledge that both historically and in the contemporary world women across cultures have been denied the political, constitutional, and legal rights guaranteed to men, despite the fact that these rights have been broadly characterized, at least lately, as human rights. Because women have been identified almost exclusively as belonging to the domestic arena, they have been disconnected from public life and isolated from mainstream structures of power. Although social, economic, and political forces have changed over time, women's association with the home and the family has remained remarkably constant. Women's role as nurturer and socializer, though socially created, has become a "universal" condition at the same time that men have succeeded in masculinizing the public arena.

Recently, there has been an impressive array of publications offering unprecedented glimpses of women's role in production, the family, the public arena, and the arts.[4] In the Middle East, as elsewhere, scholars have rewritten history and recreated the categories of inquiry. Researchers are elevating women to the rank of subject—to the realm of agents of history.[5] In a variety of different ways scholars are increasing our knowledge about social roles, women's activities, and women's relations with men. Whether employed in feminist (explaining the origins of patriarchy), Marxist (using a class analysis informed by gender), or French poststructuralist theory (drawing on psychoanalysis to account for gender identity),[6] gender is emerging as an analytic category that helps us understand how power is expressed, how society is constructed, and which roles women and men play out and why.

Historian Joan Wallach Scott has convincingly written in the context of European studies that unveiling empirical information about women invalidates the misguided notion that they have played no significant role in the past. But she cautions against marginalizing women into what she calls a "separate sphere," believing that the particularity of women needs to be examined in relation to the universality of the human experience. She argues in favor of the significance of gender as a tool for analysis, defining gender in this instance as the contradictory meanings attributed to sexual difference. Like Scott, Valentine Moghadam argues in the context of the Middle East that gender is a culturally and historically bound relational concept that assumes a connection between men and women, i.e., it is not about women only, but about the basic structural relationship between the sexes that links the state, the economy, and other processes and institutions.[7]

Just as there is no single theoretical paradigm for gender analysis, there is no one methodology. While some researchers incorporate women into standard historical categories such as labor, political parties, or nationalist movements, others challenge the very legitimacy of these categories. As the activities of both ordinary and extraordinary women are documented, investigators puzzle over whether they possess a distinct female consciousness that inspires actions or informs decisions or whether their roles as wives and mothers affect public behavior. While some assert that gender is not biologically or physically rooted but socially constructed, and that differences in status, political power, economic achievement, or educational attainment cannot be reduced to anatomical distinctions, others maintain the experience of motherhood does influence the way women behave as citizens. Sara Ruddick, for example, has advanced the idea of "maternal thinking" as a corrective to male-oriented culture; Jean Bethke Elshtain has written about "social feminism" as a way of reformulating political consciousness.[8] Ruddick and Elshtain defend the family and promote mothering as a means of understanding gender identity and female political thinking. Ruddick maintains that even the most socially powerless women in patriarchal societies possess moral authority as mothers. Since both men and women are first and foremost family beings, rather than political and economic creatures, the family becomes the fundamental arena of human life. Women, Elshtain believes, have a predisposition toward loving, empathic behavior that comes from mothering, which when translated into citizenship encourages a "politics of compassion" and an "ethical polity."

These so-called maternalists assert that women should be viewed in their capacity as mothers because of the primacy and importance of that role and argue against a definition of citizenship based on a "masculine" conception of the person as an independent, self-interested (male) being. They have tried to reformulate the concept of citizenship by establishing the moral supremacy of the family. In what appears to be a feminist about-face, they suggest that the private realm should become the archetype for citizenship and that maternal thinking must become the foundation for a new definition of power, citizenship, and the public realm. They try to humanize the way we think about politics by incorporating Nancy Chodorow's work on psychoanalytic object-relations theory and Carol Gilligan's study on moral development.[9]

Mary Dietz attacks this theory on the grounds that the maternalist construct reinforces a one-dimensional view of women as rooted in the family. Dietz asserts that the family is not a democratic institution and being a mother is not the same as being a citizen. Women who enter politics must engage with others as dispassionate citizens and not as a mother would interact with a child. She suggests that feminist consciousness best supports the political values of freedom and equality.[10] Dietz does not regard women as morally superior to men and does not think that feminists must choose between the masculine, competitive, public domain and the maternal, loving, private arena. But she does contest the maternalist view that mothering predisposes women to be empathetic.

Carole Pateman analyzes citizenship using an entirely different paradigm. She points out that European women were historically excluded from citizenship because they were believed to lack the essential male characteristics of reason and temperateness necessary for participation in political life. Because only women become pregnant, give birth, and nurse their young, they were deemed essential to the stability of the family but grossly unsuited to political activity. Their natural capacities to give birth and to mother precluded their entrance into the public worlds of government and citizenship. Even after they were given rights, albeit as subordinates, their duty to the state was framed in terms of their status as mothers. Pateman explains the politics of motherhood as an evolving concept that first excluded women from the rights and responsibilities of citizenship and then included them in the political order through their function as reproducers. Their duty to the state was based on their capacity for motherhood,[11] that is, their capacity to give birth to new citizens.

Some feminist scholars argue that rearing children, as opposed to bearing them, is a socially determined practice, and men's and women's identities, roles in society, and even prospects and purposes in life have been culturally constructed. Anthropologists, most notably Margaret Mead, looked at social developments across cultures and asserted that gender relationships were culturally, not biologically, assigned. Contending that women's lower status was not attributable to biological inferiority, she and other researchers connected women's social, legal, and political inequality to the social condition associated with their capacity to give birth.

In a similar way, this study accepts the view that gender is a culturally and socially shaped cluster of expectations, attributes, and behav-
iors assigned by a society and therefore a form of social conditioning.
As learned conduct, it is deeply felt and profoundly complex.[12] If it is
true, as Simone de Beauvoir wrote, that "one is not born, one rather
becomes a woman,"[13] then it is imperative to ask what girls learn and
how they are conditioned to accept imposed values. Catherine Mac-
Kinnon writes that gender socialization is designed to convince women
to identify themselves as sexual beings that exist for men. Since women
internalize a male image of their own sexuality, men are empowered,
women are subordinate, and sexuality becomes the key to gender inequality.[14] Men control women's sexuality both through coercion (rape
and pornography) and through laws (restrictions on abortion and
birth control). A case can be made for this proposition using Egypt as
an example, since there women's sexuality is considered so potent that
it requires control through practices such as segregation, veiling, or,
most radically, clitoridectomy. Evelyne Accad, who has written extensively on Arab society, in fact argues that a sexual revolution is needed before any society in the Middle East can be reformed. This revolution must start at the level of the family and move more broadly into
the public domain.[15]

For Scott, Pateman, Moghadam, Accad, and other scholars who understand the primacy of gender, the organization of society is premised
on the relationship between the sexes. While the role of gender and the
differences of status attributed to men and women vary within each
cultural setting, gender distinctions produce enduring social hierarchies in all societies. Not only are men's and women's places in society
affected but, for purposes of research, our own categories of analysis
also reflect these differences. When research projects mirror social hierarchies, for example, power is defined in terms of political parties,
government institutions, formal legislative offices, and the nation-
state. As Cynthia Nelson has pointed out, in a pathbreaking study, this
narrow reading erroneously implies that women have no history of political action.[16] Because war, diplomacy, and high politics are not explicitly about the relationship between men and women, gender seems
not to be relevant to them. When this view is accepted, women are separated from politics and connected only to their biological function
and the family is detached from the nation.[17] In the end women be-

come invisible, and men have reinforced the dualistic worldview of themselves as political and women as apolitical.[18]

Men have been allowed to design the world from their own point of view, establish truth according to their own version, and create the categories of citizen, leader, warrior, and worker out of their own experiences and activities. Since men have appropriated the authority to fashion the world from their own perspective, power has become male in form and in substance.[19] To become powerful, women must connect their public and private lives and unmask society's efforts to restrict their involvement. When Kate Millet coined the phrase "the personal is political" in 1970, she uncovered the political dimension of the relationship between men and women at the most intimate level and gave voice to the diverse political experiences of women in society.

When gender is understood as an epistemology, and men and women seen as joint participants in society, the interconnections between their lives can be drawn. By acknowledging the dialetics of gender, men's and women's lives are infused with equal importance and women are rescued from invisibility and obscurity. This approach to knowledge also eliminates the artificially stark dichotomies between public and private arenas, state and family, work and sexuality.

The Implications of Religious and Social Practice on Citizenship

In discussing how gender has framed Middle Eastern society, Amal Rassam describes the region as having a patrilineal-patriarchal culture with an Islamic ideology; the sexual asymmetry that results expresses itself in customs such as veiling and segregation.[20] In this region an established patriarchal tradition has merged with the Islamic faith to dictate family relations that include the man as the acknowledged head of the household, protector, and breadwinner. The woman serves him, defers to him, and accepts his guardianship.

While the status of women in Egypt cannot be solely attributed to Islam, it is important in defining women's place. Although theoretically Islam considers men and women spiritual equals, in practice it stipulates differences: women are allowed to own property and inherit family wealth, but only half as much as men. Men are favored in marriage and divorce laws and, according to the Quran, their testimony is worth twice that of a woman's. Husbands are required to protect and support their wives, children, and households financially; women are bound to attend to the needs of the family.

According to some contemporary Muslim feminist scholars, religion has institutionalized the forces that dominate women. Fatima Mernissi argues that women's citizenship is dictated by religious law, Sharia. Although today secular civil codes govern much of life in the public domain, sacred law continues to control the family and the status of women. Judges, rulers, lawyers, and social commentators continue to rely on classic commentators of *hadith* (the traditions and deeds of the Prophet), such as the still influential ninth-century historian al-Tabari, when exploring contemporary conditions. To justify men's control over women's activities, for example, conservatives might refer to Quran verse 34, which says that "men are the protectors and maintainers of women," and then to al-Tabari's commentary:

In saying that men are the protectors and maintainers of women, God Almighty established men as the guardians of their women in all of that which entails discipline and restraint and for which they are duty bound to God and to their husbands. That is because God has given more to the one than to the other. God has given more to men because they bequeath women with dowry, provide them with their needs and supply them with adequate provisions. God Almighty has therefore endowed men with superior gifts and established them as the protectors and maintainers of women, who must obey them in all affairs of their lives.[21]

For Mernissi, however, obedience is neither a virtue nor the ideal behavior to exhibit toward the family. Submission to men involves an economic quid pro quo whereby in exchange for accepting the traditional family relations stipulated by early religious officials women earn their material support from their spouses. In this construct women are viewed merely as consumers while men are praised as producers. Mernissi continues:

The relationship within the Muslim family is dominated by the leadership/obedience pattern. Obedience implies surrendering the rights of freedom and thought, opinion and expression, in other words, relinquishing to others one's free will and personal independence, which are two of the most sacred of human rights enshrined in . . . the Universal Declaration.[22]

If women were to jettison religiously inspired and traditionally maintained notions of obedience and exercise freedoms of thought, conscience, and religion as guaranteed by the Universal Declaration of Human Rights, Islamic traditionalists would consider them to be defying the faith and subverting matrimonial obligations.

Both Fatima Mernissi and Mai Ghoussoub raise the question, Why does Islam seem to regard women as being so powerfully seductive and inherently dangerous? Islam cautions men not to be tempted by *fitna*, understood dialectically as meaning beauty and turmoil, or feminine appeal and societal disorder;[23] women as sexual beings possess an insidious ability to tempt men away from their social and religious obligations. For society to function properly and according to the faith, their destructive powers must be controlled and sexual appetites restrained. Men accomplish this by providing segregated spaces for women, enforcing veiling, defending polygyny and spousal repudiation, and justifying arranged marriages. Men bestow upon themselves unconditional control over politics, the economy, religion, family decisions, and sexuality. Lacking the power to do otherwise, women accommodate themselves by directing their energies to the family, deferring to men, empowering their sons, controlling their daughters-in-law, and sometimes wearing the veil. They acknowledge that they live in a man's world, a world that is often inhospitable and threatening.

Though rarely practiced today, in theory Islam allows a man to marry up to four wives, as long as he can provide equally for each of them. In contrast to men, who live with few restrictions, women's behavior is closely monitored to ensure social harmony. Secluding women is the most extreme solution to potentially compromising situations, but a host of other constraints are imposed to counteract the assumed power of women's passions. Sexuality, in the sense Catherine MacKinnon suggests, is the real issue in Muslim society and relates to women's allegedly destructive capabilities and to men's need to contain them.

The Muslim community, or the *umma*, is required by the Sharia to establish a moral social order on earth. But as Mernissi points out, although the early umma represented an advance for women over conditions in pre-Islamic society, women's movements and freedoms were restricted. Contemporary critics of women's status in Islam, like Mernissi, argue that while the Sharia offers no real ethical codes or moral values regarding male-female relations, it treats women as sexual beings who need protection from their own immorality[24] and embodies a codified double standard whereby women are supervised and restricted while men are granted latitude in their behavior through polygyny and easy divorce rules.[25] Fatima Mernissi concludes that a fundamental contradiction exists between Islam as interpreted in official policy and equality between the sexes.[26] One cancels out the other.

Yet, Mernissi also argues that citizenship and Islam are not inherently contradictory; women's rights can be legitimized within a religious context. Islam need only be reinterpreted by scholars who accept changes in the modern age and appreciate the logic and urgency of social transformation.[27] In the current era of Muslim fundamentalist activism, however, Mernissi is unusually optimistic. Even though most Muslims are not fundamentalists, conservative social and religious arguments resonate among broad populations and dominate the way men and women presently play out their social roles. Islamists locate gender at the center of their ideology and base their views on a literal interpretation of the Sharia. They assert that social harmony and healthy family life depend upon women's commitment to husband and children, and they direct women to remain in the privacy of their homes, remote from public life. In an effort to promote conservative cultural practices, Islamists manipulate gender relations to advance their ideological and social positions. But when publicly making the case for traditional life, fundamentalists talk about God, the Prophet Muhammad, and their teachings; they do not necessarily acknowledge the centrality of gender to their arguments.

In the last few decades scholars of Middle Eastern society have condemned the simple and often hostile focus of attention on conservative Islam, identifying this trend as misguided orientalism—a methodology that conceptualizes Islam as monolithic, unchanging, and separate from the socioeconomic processes that influence behavior.[28] While it is important to sound a cautionary note in this regard, it is nevertheless indisputable that religion plays a crucial role in defining the cultural, social, and legal systems in the Middle East. Both through Islam and through the socioeconomic forces that evolved over time, men have codified their privileges and erected a hierarchal social arrangement whereby men's freedom contrasts with women's domesticity.[29]

While accepting that the absence of social and religious equality has privileged men, nevertheless Amal Rassam cautions against viewing women *merely* as victims of repression and subordination. She reminds us that women and men constantly renegotiate the rules that define and circumscribe relationships, making social life both dynamic and reciprocal as they seek to influence each other to achieve particular objectives. Despite the fact that the boundaries of women's behavior have been profoundly restricted in Egyptian society, women can still influence the conditions in which they live, work, govern, mother, and interact. To accomplish their aims they may act strategically, using domestic efficiency, for example, to offset the resentment and fear others harbor when they go outside the home to work for wages, or give up rights in the family to gain freedom in the public arena. They adapt to the changing political and religious requirements of the time—for instance most recently to the religious fundamentalism that has challenged some of the progress they have made since the beginning of the century.

In the prevailing "social contract" men established their control over both the public and private spheres. The public arena became the focus of power, privilege, and action; the private sphere was designed as politically and socially insignificant. Valid in both Western and Islamic societies, the distinctions became important because social relationships such as husband and wife, employer and worker derived from them, and because men became the only beings able to enter into contracts for themselves. According to this frame of analysis, gender relations place values and differentials on a variety of activities in society. These differentials entitle or deny people access to power, money, prestige, and position, and they contribute to the distinct roles men and women play. Women have been socialized to accept a domestic identity while men are taught to combine multiple roles.

In designing the social contract men restricted the categories of citizen, worker, and employer to themselves. They also crafted the marriage contract and became the husbands who controlled family life. Whereas men could inhabit both the public and private worlds, and even dominate both, women were governed by a social structure that enforced inequality and diminished their role and their influence. By

imposing these controls men intended to subdue women's unpre-
dictable and destructive "nature" and in the process safeguard the social order. Men's self-identified reason, sense of justice, and political
morality contrasted with women's purported passion.[30]

Egyptian men's control over women as husbands, employers, fathers, or clerics has been consolidated by the partition erected between
the public and private arenas. Relegated by their natures to the private
sphere, or "protected space," of the family and to the care of their
menfolk, women were not allowed to develop the male standard of political maturity or social sensitivity needed to function in civil society.

Mary Ann Tetreault has written that the notion of "protected
space" is an expansion of the ancient Greek distinction between the
private space of the home and the public space of politics and markets.
According to this framework, man's public actions were subject to external reviews and sanctions by peers and superiors, but what man did
in the privacy of his home was outside public scrutiny.[31] One is tempted to argue that in all human societies sexual asymmetry corresponds
to the institutional division between the domestic and public spheres
of activity, the former structured around reproduction, affective, and
familial bonds and restricted to women, the latter related to collective
social and economic activity and organized by men. While all societies
are structurally and culturally different from one another, there is com-
monality in the fact that women's position in society has been connected to their biological functions: bearing children and lactating. In
their capacity as mothers they care for the young, are responsible for
the maintenance of the home and the family,[32] and are reduced to their
"nature" by those in control of public life.

While men consider it both normal and obligatory to link work
with marriage and family, for contemporary Egyptian women this
combination exposes fundamental conflicts. To critics working wives
are akin to inadequate mothers; they also degrade their husbands' social position as breadwinners by revealing that women's wages constitute a necessary part of the family economy.

The phrase *working wives* has only recently been applied to the
Egyptian women who work for wages, and it is instructive. In this category women are identified as belonging to a family and as participating in wage labor, though both the family and the workplace remain in
men's control. No one refers to men as working husbands; the term is

as redundant as it is meaningless. Unlike women, husbands and fathers are expected to be wage earners, but they are not required to participate in household life.

Egyptian women have not been fully recognized as workers (or employees). Instead, they have been viewed first as women and only secondarily as income generating actors. Language is significant and the word *worker* holds particular importance. Carole Pateman writes that in the patriarchal paradigm a worker is a man who supports an economically dependent wife; a worker is the "breadwinner" who is valued and who has financial responsibility for the family. According to this interpretation, women's work is supplementary, secondary to men's, and considered much less significant. Categorized as wives or daughters, women are assumed to be economically dependent, and their subservience at home is the quid pro quo for their maintenance.[33]

For civil society to embrace both genders, it must be broad enough to include two sets of "individuals," one masculine and one feminine. For the categories of men/women and public/private to be transformed, they must be rebuilt with women and men as the equal architects. In this new construction biological determinism must be discarded so that a woman's position is no longer dictated by her nature. In place of "nature," social, cultural, and political considerations must prevail.[34] Since gender goes beyond the exclusive arena of the family and determines how people are included in the labor market, what kind of education they receive, what ideas they accept, and how they are incorporated into the polity, its meaning must be inclusive and equitably framed.[35]

In the final analysis, men and women can only move toward social and political equality when women are allowed to become equal to men as civil individuals.[36] Carole Pateman, Susan Moller Okin, Valentine Moghadam, and others have suggested that for women to become equal in the social arena men must become full participants in family life taking part in child rearing and other domestic tasks. The argument for change is premised on the elimination of the public and private arenas as they have been constituted and the radical reformation of the private domain.[37]

Hisham Sharabi focuses this discussion squarely on the Middle East and argues that paternal domination can only be disabled and women emancipated through a complete restructuring of the nuclear family.

Referring to the constellation of social and gender relations in the contemporary Arab world, Sharabi has adopted the term *neopatriarchy* to describe the way modern Arab society organizes itself. In the neopatriarchy, he suggests, every facet of Arab social, economic, political, and cultural life has been affected by its relationship with the West. This includes dress, food, and life styles, institutions, schools, and parliament, literature, philosophy, and science. According to this paradigm, Middle Eastern society developed in a dependent and distorted fashion because of its subordinated relationship with the colonialist world. While the trappings of Western modernity have been incorporated into Arab society, schizophrenic and insecure attitudes have kept the Middle East traditional at its core and fundamentally hostile to change.[38]

Family life has been especially resistant to reorganization, according to Sharabi. It has entitled the father to maintain his authority over his wife and children and restrict women to the role of childbearer and child rearer. Sharabi's understanding of male domination is consistent with the definition of patriarchy forwarded by Zillah Eisenstein, who argues that patriarchy is the sexual and economic struggle between men and women to control women's lives in order to keep their role as mother primary. Eisenstein believes that while it is the biological assignment of women to bear children, it is the political assignment of women to rear them.[39] Men's power rests with their ability to define women's choices and is reinforced by the ideology and laws of the state, which legitimate the notion that women function best as mothers outside the public arena.

The dynamics of the family change, Sharabi notes, through economic transformation and industrialization, increased education for girls and boys, and greater employment opportunities for women. Valentine Moghadam adds that the configuration of family life can be altered through state legal reform and the efforts of popular social movements.[40] Both theorists call for democratic development within the family.

Sharabi argues for expanded economic opportunities for women as a precondition to their liberation;[41] Moghadam stresses the need for increased education. Based on studies done by the United Nations, upon which Moghadam relies, increasing educational opportunities for women have changed their self-image, broadened their expectations, and led to a recent decline in early marriage.[42] Ultimately, women's self-identification must be broadened to include not only that of family member but also that of worker, employer, and citizen. In order for this to be accomplished in Egypt the personal status/Muslim family laws through which men continue to maintain their control over their female relatives must be eliminated. But the abolition of legal and social restrictions requires a transformation of attitudes that is difficult to achieve, especially in the current ideological context where conservative religious fundamentalism has gained ground.

Small groups of women in Egypt have challenged the social discourse that has identified them as weak and needing protection and, through political organization, have tried to shatter what Kathleen Jones has termed the "sexual iconography" of the community. This kind of psychological and social insurgency can profoundly change society, break down what has been a resilient public/private dichotomy, and end the politics of exclusion. Women's marginalized status in the political community ends when the norms of political behavior are no longer represented as masculine.[43] The question of who belongs and who does not belong to a community is where the politics of citizenship begins.

Despite the fact that Egyptian women have participated in community life through social networking, nurturing families, rural and urban employment, and national politics, their activities have been devalued and the terms of their citizenship have suffered. In contrast to men, who have always been expected to undertake the political tasks associated with citizenship, neither the extension of the vote to women in 1956, their membership in political and social organizations, nor their election to public office has transformed women into accepted political actors. Politics continues to be a man's business and government remains their territory.[44] As long as politics, work, and manhood are fused in people's minds, and womanhood and nature inextricably linked, women can not function as equal citizen members of the community, and equality will remain elusive.[45] Before women can move from the identity of daughter/wife/mother to citizen, perceptions must change and cultural biases jettisoned.

Cultural presuppositions are the bedrock of society and are embraced by both men and women. Developed over long periods of time and maintained as truths, they are complex in nature and stubbornly resistant to change. Like females across the globe, Egyptian women are often, ironically, the strongest supporters of the customs that limit their own lives.[46] In an interview with *Al-Ahram Weekly*, activist and family planning advocate Aziza Hussein argued that the greatest obstacle to women's progress is cultural.

> The crucial problem is that Egyptian women do not think for themselves; it is always men who think and act on their behalf. This attitude deprives women of intellectual progress, it makes them cocooned and feel threatened. . . . Women are always hesitant to assume a role. Even within the family where women shoulder most of the responsibilities, they are still unable to act as decision makers.[47]

Carole Pateman's argument that the patriarchal family is no school for democratic citizenship[48] and Hisham Sharabi's view that legal and social constraints imposed on women can be altered by introducing egalitarian modes of raising children and organizing family relations are highly compelling positions.[49] Both agree that the private arena of the family is where societal reorganization must originate. The family is a microcosm of society; it embraces members who teach and practice values, learn and replicate behavior, and shape the roles assumed in public life. If women continue to be silenced at home, they will also be rejected in public company. Societies that continue to identify citizenship rights with the gender-specific behavior of men disempower women and weaken political and social life.

A reconceptualization of citizenship is necessary for women to become genuine members of the society. This will require the satisfaction of two radical elements: people must be seen as individuals rather than as representatives of a particular gender, and the private sphere must be reformed and a practice of democracy installed. Women ought not be social exiles. To become autonomous citizens they must redefine their status as protected, dependent, and subordinate females.[50]

CHAPTER TWO | Liberalism, Nationalism, and Gender

BEGINNING AT THE END OF the nineteenth century, Egyptian social life began to change as the country was drawn into the capitalist world market with resulting secularization, urbanization, and technological developments.[1] These changes influenced gender relations, especially among the upper classes, and altered the way households were organized. In particular, harem life and polygyny, hitherto common among the urban rich, began to disappear. The harem, according to Margot Badran, had two associations: it indicated the part of the house that upper-class women and children occupied and it referred to the wife or number of wives a man maintained. Until then men and women of the upper and middle classes in the cities led strictly separate lives. Women spent most of their time in the female quarters of the home. When they emerged to go to the public bath or visit relatives, for example, they covered their faces to retain the bounds of separation.[2] Females wore the veil from about the age of nine to conceal their individual identity and as a form of protection. The veil distinguished them as members of the upper class and they became, therefore, untouchable to men to whom they were unrelated.

In the cities secluded women were evidence of a man's wealth and prestige. Prosperous Egyptians constructed ornate dwellings filled with lavish furnishings equipped with comfortable and spacious women's quarters where women could enjoy the company of eunuchs (castrated men who had been taken as slaves from Sudan) who entertained them and acted as buffers to the outside world. In contrast, the poor of both sexes shared the same limited space in the home, though poor women were also veiled when they went out in the world. Arguably, ordinary women were marginally freer than their affluent sisters since they went about the neighborhood and some worked as soothsayers, dressmakers, servants, and midwives.

While Jewish and Christian women were not segregated in their households, they too donned the veil when they ventured outdoors. Generations of Jews, Armenians, Greeks, and Italians had been born in Egypt but remained largely unassimilated into its culture. A significant number still held European passports, traveled abroad, and were culturally attached to Western society. While these communities were small, they were usually prosperous. Foreigners were most apt to be businessmen, teachers, translators, shopkeepers, or skilled workers.[3]

Until the middle of the twentieth century most women spent their time at home and within the neighborhood in the company of other women to whom they were related patrilineally. Mothers, daughters, sisters, aunts, and cousins associated together in a family compound or a local community where they protected and supported one another. They relied on this close family network to rescue a member who suffered economic hardship, mediate family conflicts, and serve as marriage councilors. They were the closest of friends and, sometimes, the bitterest of enemies, but this was the world they inhabited and the people with whom they felt the most secure.

Men were rarely allowed into, or entered, the society of women where female bonds and common experiences solidified relations and maintained cohesion. Women and girls participated in and perpetuated female rituals such as dying the hands, face, and hair with henna (especially during times of celebration), ear piercing, and female circumcision. They explored issues considered too sensitive to discuss with spouses, such as family planning and birth control, relied on one another for emotional support, and sought advice that they regularly heeded.

Men and women from across the social classes still accepted the traditional and centuries-old matrimonial arrangements whereby elder members of the family orchestrated a match, often between cousins or blood relations, solidifying family, village, or neighborhood ties. Couples seldom met before their wedding day and rarely opposed the will of parents. Divorce was rare and granted to women only on the grounds of male insanity, impotence, or nonmaintenance. But a man had a unilateral right to divorce, as stated in the Quran, and only had to declare, three times, "I divorce you" if he chose to invoke this privilege. This power gave men substantial authority over their wives since Egyptian culture looked with great disfavor upon divorced women, who were considered burdens by fathers or brothers obliged to support them.[4]

In Egypt, a rigidly stratified society until Abd al-Nasir came to power in 1952, a few rich and powerful families controlled the vast majority of Egyptians, the rural *fallahin,* who lived in primitive conditions and suffered from debilitating diseases such as tuberculosis, malnutrition, and trachoma. Agriculture provided the main source of sustenance for the country's inhabitants. The Nile River fertilized the land, provided its material security, and was the center of its rituals, celebrations, and traditions. Peasant women regularly worked alongside their men in the fields, and because of the backbreaking labor they performed could not be encumbered by restrictive clothing. Not only did they toil barefaced, but they walked about the community unveiled because the villagers regarded each other as extended family. Villagers could therefore move around more openly than their counterparts in the city.

Urban girls from prosperous families were given some schooling, from the end of the nineteenth century, in keeping with the fashionable idea that female education was important to the well-being of the family and to the progress of the nation. Some late nineteenth- and early twentieth-century reformers were genuinely interested in improving the status of women, others were committed to the development of society and women and girls were judged useful to the national interest.[5]

The government founded the Siyufiyah School, the first state school for girls in 1873, on the recommendation of Tcheshme Hanim, one of the wives of Khedive Ismail (1863–1872). The new school, which attracted the daughters of the Muslim Egyptian and Turkish ruling class as well as their young concubines, had enrolled four hundred students by the end of its first year. Parenthetically, for centuries it had been quite common for high officials in Egypt to bring into their harems white Circassian female slaves from the eastern shore of the Black Sea. While some affluent men married these girls, others kept them as concubines. Regardless of their legal positions, slave girls enhanced the prestige of a man's household and were regarded as a sign of status. It was not unusual for these girls to be educated in the newly established state schools.

At about the same time the government also established the Saniyah School, which instituted a teachers' training program. Several additional schools had been established in Cairo and Alexandria by 1916, but female education developed slowly. By 1920 there were five government primary schools for girls; in 1925 the first secondary school for girls was established; and in 1928 a small number of women were admitted to Cairo University. Six of them were enrolled in the university's medical faculty and a handful of others in the faculty of arts and sciences; all were graduates of the private foreign school system, which existed alongside the state structure, established by European missionaries throughout the Middle East.

Small groups of upper-class women began to undertake social welfare projects and public philanthropy during this era and to organize gatherings for their intellectual and social development. In particular, they established medical associations to provide health information and hygiene to poor women, founded literacy classes for working-class girls,[6] and set up literary salons where they discussed essays, literary pieces, and political treatises, some of which they had written themselves. Using a feminist voice, some upper-class women began to speak about and others to write about female education, employment, polygyny, marriage, divorce, and political rights. An exclusively female press existed at this time and was an ideal vehicle for their ideas. Conscious of the restrictions placed upon them because of their gender, and mindful of the privileges their social class provided, they called for changes in the organization of society. By engaging in a discussion about conditions of life in the family and about the importance of establishing new roles for women in the civic arena, they pushed the boundaries of convention and insisted on a more public profile.[7]

The Roots of Liberalism in Egypt

When Great Britain occupied Egypt in 1882 the country was still part of the Ottoman Empire. From the outset Egyptians deeply resented the British occupation. In 1919 they staged a nationalist revolution in which activists from across class, geographic, and gender lines fought the British for local control of their country. Women joined the rebellion, and male activists endorsed their limited participation in the liberation struggle. "Nationalism, in Egypt as elsewhere in the Arab world, was the key to the legitimacy of the women's movement in the eyes of both politicians and the public," writes Sarah Graham-Brown.[8] But, as later actions in the postindependence period demonstrate, men tolerated women's activity only to the extent that it furthered national politics and did not support broad-based political action.

Following the breakup of the Ottoman Empire, the failed nationalist revolution of 1919, and decades of fruitless negotiations between Cairo and the colonial authorities, Britain unilaterally granted Egypt limited independence in 1922. During the liberal era that followed, the Egyptians fashioned a political system based on a Western-style constitution and drawn up by Egyptian legal experts who were sympathetic to British tradition and parliamentary government. The framers of the constitution sought to limit the strength of the nationalist forces that remained after the 1919 revolution and to introduce a form of liberal self-government into the country. The two-chamber parliament, consisting of a senate and chamber of deputies,[9] was constituted with members elected through universal male suffrage, aside from two-fifths of the Senate reserved for direct appointment first by King Fuad (1917–1936) and then by his son King Faruk (1936–1952). The monarchy, jealous of its power, periodically compromised the liberal experiment by illegitimately unseating nationalist prime ministers and replacing them with undesirable palace favorites.

Despite independence and the introduction of liberalism, Great Britain continued to control the country's economic, military, and political affairs. As a result, throughout the liberal period nationalism dominated Egypt's political culture, serving as a cover for local conservative parliamentary leaders to resist putting social and economic reform on the agenda. Even the Wafd, the premier liberal organization in the country and unquestionably the most socially progressive of the mainstream parties, ignored the poor and marginalized women's rights.

While liberalism and early feminism did provide affluent women limited space and legitimacy in which to engage in nationalist politics, help the poor through voluntary social service projects, and enter the literary arena, the vast majority of women remained outside public life and held no rights of citizenship. Nor did they ever question the prevailing social structure from which they derived sociopsychological rewards.[10] In Egypt, where conservative social traditions predominated, the core principles of liberalism were compromised when women were denied the right to vote, stand for political office, or otherwise contribute to national policy, as men retained the authority to enact and enforce laws.

Egyptian liberalism derived from classic European traditions that dated back to the seventeenth and eighteenth centuries. At that time Western political thinkers articulated a new order based on secularism, representative rule, limited government, and a system of checks and balances. Over time, as liberalism evolved, it incorporated capitalist economic planning and social welfare policies into its jurisdiction and included individual rights, the free market, liberty, and personal privacy. Liberalism institutionalized the separation between the public and private spheres of life. The state, being prohibited from intruding into people's lives, had virtually no impact upon the relations between men and women in the family.

In this construction the male public sphere was entirely separated from the private world of the family where women belonged.[11] Patriarchy became a form of power where women were excluded from becoming civil individuals and where they never emerged from their "nonage" and from the protection of men. Even with the passage of time and the gaining of legal and political rights women never entirely managed to overcome this confinement, and they did not interact in civil society on the same basis as men.[12]

In the early European liberal era and in Egypt's semiliberal society women remained outside the mainstream of power and subordinated to men in both public and private life. Liberalism's advocates successfully posited the ideological dichotomy between the private/personal and the public/political whereby a hierarchy of power assigned a subordinate place to women based on their natural role as childbearers. While women were exclusively linked to the private domain, men were expected to be heads of household with power over wives and children and to take their place in civil life.[13]

Liberalism in Egypt was structured such that men and women did not enjoy equality in society. Socialized into particular roles with distinct interests and separate status, women were deemed unqualified for the demands of citizenship and unable to transcend their bodily natures and sexual passions; men were expected to carry out the duties and responsibilities of public life because they used reason, developed a sense of justice, upheld universal civil law, and sublimated their passions. By overcoming nature men acquired the competence and maturity needed to function in the public arena.[14]

Women's experiences, temperaments, and sensibilities differed from those of men, and since the male standard of activity and conduct became the model, women were considered ill suited to the duties regularly performed by men. This was even true after women gained legal equality and after political systems were theoretically premised on the concept of universality. Although institutions, language, rules, laws, and customs claimed to be general, in actuality, they were gender-based and hierarchical.[15] As Carole Pateman asserts, while equality allows for differences among people, there is no democratic citizenship when any one group is subordinated to another. Within a truly democratic polity men and women must be full citizens and their citizenship must be of equal worth to both.

Civil society functions best in a democracy according to agreed upon political rules, civic and organizational diversity, and popular participation in voluntary autonomous organizations such as professional clubs, tolerant religious groups, independent trade unions, women's associations, charitable societies, and social fellowships. Civil society incorporates diverse organizations, tolerates minority rights, and limits the arbitrary exercise of state authority.[16] The individual is allowed to emerge when people are encouraged to participate in political and social life.

Civil processes existed in only rudimentary form in liberal-age Egypt. The political system was urban-based, colonially imposed, and unrepresentative of the masses in society. Elites dominated the urban and rural populations, who were powerless and separated from cosmopolitan centers of cultural and political life.[17] There were many political parties, periodic elections, parliamentary sessions, and differing degrees of freedom of the press and association, but the constitution was also regularly abrogated because elite political parties did not act as a brake on the excessive powers of the king. Civil society was weakened by rural and urban upper-class leaders who were fearful of the potential power of the masses and deliberately contained them. Although the political leadership introduced liberal institutions and concepts of Western representative democracy into the country, they did not transmit the cultural values consistent with liberalism. In particular, because they never accepted the importance of individual rights,[18] the liberal democratic experiment was severely and deliberately jeopardized.

From a gendered perspective the basic principles of liberty and individual rights were defined when Egyptian constitutionalists excluded women from full political participation. Women were denied the right to vote, to hold office, or to make public policy, despite the role they had played in the 1919 nationalist revolution. They were deprived of social, political, and legal privileges because they were viewed as irrational, apolitical, and naturally different. Because political parties and institutions belonged to men, particularly to upper-class men, and because the ideal Egyptian citizen fit a particular male profile, women were distanced from mainstream sources of power and excluded from rights and responsibilities in public life. Equality became a selectively applied principle and not a practice generally exercised.[19]

The relevance of gender to the construction of liberal society was explicit since women were categorized as wives and mothers, perceived as capable of acting only in the narrow interests of their family, and dismissed as unfit for citizenship or politics. Generally adopting the political opinions of their men, the majority of women muted their own opinions and contributed to the status quo of the polis.[20]

Egyptian liberalism, like its European counterpart, incorporated into itself a contradiction between the ideals of autonomy, for men, in the public sphere, and the assumption that women are naturally subject to men in the family. Egyptian liberalism merged with patriarchy to separate the public and private arenas. Its framers conferred public life, the world of politics, markets, administration, and culture upon men and denied women the rights of citizenship.[21]

Because of gender asymmetry men controlled not only the public affairs of the state but also the family as husbands and fathers. The result was particularly insidious since women were acutely oppressed in the private arena of the home. Consistent with classic liberal philosophy and in accordance with Islamic law that covers family relations, the state did not interfere in private life. By preserving the preexisting social conservatism of the family, constitutionalists and religious leaders maintained male dominance. Although early feminists tried to mitigate the abuses of gender inequality, their impact was restricted by their small numbers and by the unlimited authority mustered by their opponents.

Echoing the question Ursula Vogel asked in another context: Why were women denied membership in the community when they were not minors, mentally deficient, or criminals? One simple response is that women were shut out from active participation in the community because they were not men.[22] In essence, since half the population was deliberately denied civil and political rights because it was female, gender made a difference to the meaning of citizenship during the liberal era.

Patriarchal Liberalism and Civil Society

The Egyptian political elite had imported European liberal democracy into the country without shaping it to local realities of social and political life. The British continued to interfere in its politics and the king continued to wield considerable power. Even local Egyptian leaders, who feared the potential of a mass uprising and resisted involving the popular classes in the political process, never grappled with the question how liberal the liberal democratic system should be.

Not only did the occupation and the antidemocratic tendencies of the monarchy weaken constitutionalism and any movement in the direction of democracy and civil rights but the economic and political conditions posed additional difficulties as well: the economy was dominated by foreign capitalists whose commanding presence prevented the emergence of an indigenous and independent middle class. The absence of a local bourgeosie able to defend constitutionalism against agrarian landlords impeded its development. A conscious working class active in labor unions and capable of articulating political demands was yet to evolve, and the feminist movement was weakened by the inequalities dictated by politics and religion. Separated from the popular classes by culture, class origin, education, expectations, and sometimes even language, the political elite also discouraged mass participation; parties essentially expressed their own views and were not structured to incorporate a broad membership.

Four groups competed for power and alternately controlled the country: the palace, the British, the Wafd, and the so-called minority parties—the Liberal Constitutionalists, the Saadists, the People's Party, and the Unity Party. Of these the Wafd at times won the support of most of the nation at polling stations and at protests and marches; the minority parties were little more than the expression of the dominant personality who controlled them.

Although the 1923 constitution called for elections, the struggle for political power was often fought in an antidemocratic manner. A typical pattern existed in Egyptian politics: whenever a free election was held the Wafd would invariably win an overwhelming victory, then conflict with the British or the palace would predictably lead to the resignation or dismissal of the Wafd, the dissolution of Parliament, and the suspension or modification of the constitution. The Wafd was then forced into the opposition where it remained until a disagreement between the palace and a minority party, or a decision by the British, caused the Wafd to return to power. The constitutional system was thus continually challenged by autocratic politicians, domineering monarchs, and the interfering British.

With the exception of national independence, there were few subjects on which the Egyptian political leadership could agree. Attempts to negotiate independence with the British failed in 1924, 1927, and 1929–1930. It took an international crisis in the form of the Italian invasion of Ethiopia in 1936 to convince Britain to compromise. King Fuad was suspected of pro-Italian sympathies and by that time fascist Italy controlled Ethiopia and Libya. The Italians therefore posed a real threat to the region, so the British finally had to reach a settlement in Cairo. In 1936 the principals signed the historic Anglo-Egyptian Treaty, a defense pact, which recognized Egypt as an independent and sovereign nation but stipulated that Britain would aid Egypt in an emergency and that Egypt must grant Britain the military facilities needed to protect British lines of communication. Although the treaty was supported by most Egyptians, it was rejected by the religious right and the antifascist left, both of whom objected to the prospect of British troops remaining in the country for another twenty years.

In the mid-1930s world depression had undermined the appeal of the capitalist system. The liberal parties in Egypt were also being challenged by small left-wing intellectual groups and religious conservatives. The Muslim Brotherhood, Young Egypt, and socialist and communist groups organized tenacious adherents who were detached from mainstream politics and captured by emergent philosophies. Their activism intensified during World War II, especially because of the presence of hundreds of thousands of allied troops in Egypt.

Although the government remained officially neutral until February 1945, when it finally declared war against the Axis powers, Egypt made important contributions to the Allied effort. In return Egyptian nationalists hoped to be rewarded by independence when the war ended. Negotiations were renewed, but no agreement was reached. As a result, the masses became more militant throughout the latter 1940s: large demonstrations, paralyzing strikes, angry marches, and other protests against the status quo were common. The Egyptians seized the Suez Canal zone where British military installations and thousands of soldiers remained, and the situation turned violent: workers, students, intellectuals, and soldiers demonstrated against the government and closed down universities and factories. Protesters set fire to foreign businesses, hotels, department stores, cinemas, and nightclubs. Cairo was set ablaze, and the Wafdist government fell. Four governments tried to stabilize the country; each was unsuccessful. On July 23, 1952, low-level military officers led by Abd al-Nasir staged a coup d'état directed against the British, the corrupt Egyptian ruling class, and Western-style liberalism. In place of liberalism the Nasirists instituted a state-controlled system of government.[23]

That men and women engaged in public activity during the liberal era reflected their increasing political sophistication and their rising aspirations. For women, who were denied the legal rights and privileges of liberalism, involvement in feminist organizations, social welfare activity, and literary careers demonstrated their determination to be active in public life. Despite liberalism's indifference to women's activism and its affirmative resistance to altering the conditions of life in the family, women inserted themselves into Egypt's political culture. They were not passive recipients of political and ideological dogma. Rather, through their own organizations they became active on the margins of political life where they were permitted to operate. Coming initially from elite families and espousing a combination of feminism and nationalism, male rulers generally tolerated their opinions.

Because liberalism failed to produce representative government, political freedom, and civil rights for women, they created their own political life parallel to and separate from mainstream political forces. Regardless of the prohibitions against them, they developed their own leadership, goals, and strategies of operation and practiced a form of politics in as meaningful a way as they were allowed.

Feminism, Nationalism, and Political Action

During the liberal era gender relations advanced in stages. From the late nineteenth century until World War II advocates for women's rights were drawn from two very different constituencies: religious men from the Islamic reformist community and women from both the native Egyptian elite and the Turco-Circassian upper class. As advocates of social change, they separately called for revisions in Islamic family law as well as an expansion in educational and employment opportunities for girls and women. While men were inspired by religious law and changes taking place abroad, women focused on local conditions. Blending nationalism with feminism and incorporating Islam into their discourse in order to legitimize their calls for change, they organized an independent feminist movement characterized by social homogeneity and ideological cohesion.

The destabilizing events of World War II produced the second period of changing gender relations. Middle-class women challenged the old guard by joining the feminist movement and giving it a new and more militant voice. Not only did they articulate a more radical version of feminism, they also used increasingly aggressive tactics to accomplish their goals. They demanded the vote, political representation in Parliament, changes in the socioeconomic system that undermined their status in society, and reform of personal status law.

While Europe was industrializing, democratizing, and conquering much of the world economically and militarily in the nineteenth century, Egyptian intellectuals founded an Islamic reform movement that asserted Arab society was capable of overcoming its stagnation and renewing itself within the context of Islam. They also advocated the abolition of female illiteracy, seclusion, and polygyny, but this did not mean they were committed to female liberation or women's human rights. Early attempts to improve women's lives in Egypt did not involve the implementation of universalist Enlightenment ideals, as women's partial and indeed fragile citizenship status suggests. The Islamic reformers' goal was to modernize Muslim society to allow the notable political, economic, and social advances Europe was achieving, and since they considered the prevailing position of women to be antithetical to modern life, they regarded change as necessary.[24] Women were seen as vital to national progress and assigned the responsibility of reforming the next generation. Because notions of change were inspired by patriarchal assumptions, they were not especially auspicious for women's rights.

Even before the liberal era debate about women's place in modern society had led to the promotion by the state of new educational and work opportunities for women, especially in midwifery and teaching. The government's policies in this area were supported by intellectuals such as Shaykh Ahmad Rifai, Rifaa al-Tahtawi, and Ali Pasha Mubarak, who published books in 1869, 1872, and 1875, respectively, arguing that the state should instruct girls and women. Al-Tahtawi especially, influenced by the Enlightenment ideas of Voltaire, Rousseau, and Montesquieu while studying in France, became an important pioneer in women's education and women's rights.[25]

Social and religious reformers, including the notable Shaykh Muhammad Abduh (1849–1905), carried on the tradition of Islamic revival initiated by Jamal al-Din al-Afghani (1838–1897), which also advocated educational and legal improvements, the emancipation of women, economic development, and governmental reorganization that would allow Egypt to face the technological and economic changes taking place in the Western world. For Islamic reformers and even liberal nationalists the problem was—and for many remains—how to reconcile traditional culture with the modern world.[26] Arguing that the Sharia or Islamic law could be reinterpreted according to the needs of the day, the reformers declared that although the rules of Islam were unchanging their interpretation in terms of social conventions was open to modification according to circumstance. This led Abduh to the belief that Islam was fully compatible with modern thought and relevant to contemporary life. He supported educational and legal reforms for women and was critical of polygyny, which he regarded as having an adverse affect on family life.

One of Abduh's disciples, Qasim Amin, extended his mentor's ideas and gave them a more radical social orientation. In *The Liberation of Women* (1899) Amin connected the deterioration of Islamic society to the inferior status given to women. For progress to be realized, he contended, women needed education, employment, and respect, achievable within the context of Islam because it was a religion that recognized the equality of both sexes before God. He disputed the argument that the Quran required women to veil and seclude themselves, and he denounced polygyny and men's easy access to divorce. Amin believed that the progress of the nation depended on improving women's status, but he stopped short of calling for parity between the sexes. He did not, for example, advocate full participation of women in the affairs of state or suggest that they be granted political rights.

At the time his ideas were controversial. In *The New Woman* (1901), the book he wrote in response to conservative critics who had lodged an attack against him, his argument was based not on religion but on the doctrine of natural rights and the idea of progress. Signaling his ideological shift toward Western culture and secularism and his respect for the advances achieved in the West, Amin declared that women had a right to higher education in preparation for professional careers, either in "cases of need" when women were unmarried, widowed, or childless or "to benefit the family." He presumed that because women and men were intellectual and spiritual equals women had a "natural right" to an education and to participate in society, and he suggested that all Arab societies should improve the status of women to the extent accomplished in Europe.[27]

Amin's critique of society was informed by the lives of upper-class women since most peasant women worked alongside their men in the fields and since women in the city who worked for wages became wet nurses, lacemakers, dressmakers, fortune-tellers, exorcists, public bath cleaners, bookkeepers, dancers, musicians, and prostitutes.[28]

In Amin's books the reader can trace the evolution of an intellectual whose ideas gradually changed over time. Between the publication of his first book, *The Egyptians* (1894), and his later works, Amin's beliefs matured. Responding to an attack on Egypt leveled by a Frenchman, Amin argued in *The Egyptians* that female seclusion did not lead to inequality, that polygyny was practiced only in times of need, and that divorce was a personal issue between husband and wife and had no place in the court system. By the time he wrote *The Liberation of Women* these views had changed dramatically. Nadia Hijab attributes the reasoning in his first book to "cultural loyalty": Amin was very likely defending his culture against the criticisms of an outsider, adhering to the idea once put forth by Leila Ahmed that cultural allegiance accounted for Islam's hold over its members.[29] Amin's first work revealed the sensitivity of an Egyptian to criticism from a Westerner, especially in light of the prurient interest Europeans had in Arab women, which led him to a adopt a defensive posture toward foreigners.

Amin's work was widely debated and severely criticized by traditional religious leaders who disapproved of the emancipation of women and condemned any form of Western thought making its way into Islamic Egypt. Conservative lower- and middle-class nationalists also rejected his ideas. In favor of cultural authenticity, they argued that Arab society must withstand foreign assault and would only advance by drawing on local traditions of which women, as protectors of the family and carriers of religion, were an important support. Women, as standard bearers, represented the dignity of the country, but they needed guidance and supervision.

This debate over women's rights coincided with the establishment of colonial rule in the late nineteenth century. The most ardent female supporters of gender reform therefore based their arguments not only on religious but also on nationalist grounds.[30] At this time well-connected women such as Aisha Ismat al-Taimuriyya (1840–1902) and Zainab Fawwaz (1860–1914) began expanding the role and public space available to them by engaging in what had started as a male discussion of women's place in society. Zainab Fawwaz was born in Lebanon and migrated with her family to Alexandria where she studied rhetoric, published poetry, and composed essays on the right of women to education and employment. In an article entitled "Fair and Equal Treatment," written in 1892 for the publication *Al-Nil*, she argued:

> Woman was not created in order to remain within the household sphere, never to emerge. Woman was not created to become involved in work outside the home only when it is directly necessary for household management, childrearing, cooking, kneading bread, and other occupations of the same sort. . . .
>
> If we were to regard the poor women we have in Cairo, Alexandria, and all parts of Egypt, we would find most of them pursuing work just like the men. Among these women are merchants, crafts workers, and those working with male labourers in construction. . . .
>
> The persistence of woman in demanding advancement until she obtains her rights is not to be considered a crime. Rather,

posterity will glorify her, and she will be remembered with words of gratitude for opening the door of success to her sisters.[31]

Unlike the overwhelming majority of men and women of her time and even after, Zainab Fawwaz recognized the productive role women played and demanded their independence from an exclusively family-oriented identity. She held remarkably advanced opinions for the time.

Aisha Ismat al-Taimuriyya was born in Cairo, the daughter of a Circassian concubine and a high Egyptian official. She was privately tutored and became an accomplished writer who used both prose and poetry to speak out for women's rights. In a treatise written in 1894–95, entitled "Family Reform Comes Only Through the Education of Girls," she wrote:

> How regrettable is a society which has not examined the west's admirable arrangement with respect to men and women, and has made no effort to strive for the elevated dignity which this arrangement confers. How astounding is a civilisation infatuated with adorning its young women in costume jewellery. . . . But in fact this civilisation has cast those girls into the pit of evil. . . .
>
> If the male authorities strove for the improvement of these girls' behaviour through their education . . . these belles would then find themselves crowned with the rubies of knowledge. . . .
>
> This is a letter from one of the women who regards the education of girls as an obligatory duty.[32]

In 1892 a women's journal was established in Egypt by Hind al-Nawfal (ca. 1860–1920), and literate women used it to air their feminist ideas.[33] By the end of the century four women's journals had been founded in which women published their thoughts on family, social, and gender issues. One of them, Malak Hifni Nasif (1868–1918), was among the new breed of women's advocates. Using the pen name Bahithat al-Badiya (Searcher in the Desert), Nasif published a collection of articles and speeches entitled *Al-Nisaiyat* (meaning women's or feminist essays) through the press of *Al-Jarid*, the liberal nationalist newspaper of the Umma Party.[34] Both the Umma Party of the pre–World War I period and its offshoot, the Liberal Constitutionalist Party of Ahmad Lutfi al-Sayyid, supported limited women's rights as one aspect of European liberalism. They criticized laws unfavorable to women in matters of marriage, divorce, polygyny, and the lack of education available to girls, but they were not in a strong enough position in society to effect change.

In her book Nasif argued for expanded education and employment opportunities and for implementing all the rights Islam guaranteed to women. She supported a woman's right to work and not just in "lowly occupations." Noting that foreign women already worked in Egyptian schools and health care services, she asserted that cultural and national dignity required that Egyptian women provide these for themselves. She did not attribute the division of labor by gender to religious law, arguing, "Had Adam chosen cooking and washing, and Eve to work to provide support, then that would have been the system followed today."[35]

Malak Hifni Nasif graduated from the girls' section of the Abbas School in 1901, received a teacher training diploma from the Saniyah School in 1905, and taught at the Abbas School until 1907 when, as a young woman, she was married to a bedouin chief in Fayyum in southern Egypt.[36] When she joined her husband in the oasis southwest of Cairo, she learned, for the first time, that he was already married and the father of a daughter whom she was expected to tutor. Out of her own sad and torturous experience she began to write and to give speeches. Her 1909 essay, "Bad Deeds of Men: Injustice," is an indictment of polygyny. Talking about a man who took another wife, she wrote:

> When [the man] married the other woman he broke the heart of his first wife. . . . This cruel husband is criminal under the rule of law, decency, humanity, and kindness. . . .
>
> I do not believe that there is any opponent who is weaker in weaponry than us, and less vengeful. Oh God, inspire the men of our government to do right because their injustice to the nation has many repercussions on us. It seems that we have not received anything more than men receive except pain. This reverses the Quranic verse that says, "One man's share shall equal two women's shares."[37]

Malak Hifni Nasif did not keep her thoughts about the social structure of society to herself; she sent a list of demands to the Egyptian National Congress meeting outside Cairo in Heliopolis in 1911. Her ten-point program for the improvement of women's lives included the need for universal elementary education for girls with an emphasis on religious education, the expansion of employment opportunities for women, reform of the personal status laws, including the elimination of polygyny, the right of women to pray in mosques, and the need for women to train as doctors and teachers. She was not allowed to read her fifteen-minute speech directly, since women would not have been allowed to appear before Congress, so a proxy, Ahmad Mustafa, presented it to the delegates.

Malak Hifni Nasif's statement was brought up for debate on the last day of the congressional session. Her demand that women be allowed to enter the mosque separately from men, pray by themselves, and listen to sermons generated intense discussion but in the end was flatly rejected, as were her demands for an end to polygyny and easy divorce. The congressmen were more tolerant of her idea that religious education be made mandatory in girls' schools and approved her suggestions for strengthening Islamic culture. But they resisted any reform of the personal status laws. Since the congress had no legislative power, it could not have legislated reforms in any case.[38]

Like Malak Hifni Nasif, Nabawiyya Musa (1890–1951) was a published author and a graduate of the Saniyah School, herself a teacher. When she had graduated from her teachers' training program Nabawiyya Musa petitioned the Ministry of Education for permission to sit for the state baccalaureate exam, which at that time was administered only to boys. After considerable discussion she was given permission and she prepared for the test at home. She acquitted herself well by scoring in the top third of the group. In her subsequent professional life Musa taught at the Egyptian University's section for women, set up and administered her own school, and was named the first female inspector in the Ministry of Education, a post from which she was later dismissed for criticizing the girls' curriculum. She was also a founding member of the Egyptian Feminist Union (EFU) and served as a delegate to the International Woman Suffrage Alliance Conference in Rome in 1923, the first such international meeting where Egyptian feminists were represented.[39]

In her essay, "The Difference Between Men and Women and Their Capacities for Work," Musa contested the notion of biological determinism and argued that gender was a socially constructed category:

Men have spoken so much of the differences between men and
women that they would seem to be two separate species. . . .
Human beings are animals governed by the same rules of nature
regarding reproduction, growth, decline, and death. The male an-
imal is no different from the female except in reproduction. . . .

It is not true that the man is more intelligent than the woman
because his body is larger and stronger. If this were true the ge-
niuses and philosophers of this world would have had the largest
bodies. . . .

[A women] can do everything a man can, the way a short, slim
man can do what a big, tall man does. Asserting that nature has
destined the woman for the house because she is weaker than the
man this is patently untrue.[40]

Musa was a champion of gender equality, believing that if women
acquired the same qualifications as men they would be treated equally
in society. In particular, she was among the first to demand the same
wage that male teachers were receiving, thus establishing the model of
equal pay for equal work. Musa was also unconventional in her personal life: when she found out that the Ministry of Education would
not employ a married woman as a teacher, she refused to marry. Over
time Musa came to believe that married life humiliated women and she
never submitted to it.[41]

Although elite women took the lead in this early period of nationalist and feminist activity, during the 1919 Egyptian revolution women
from all social classes were active in mass demonstrations and marches. Schoolgirls distributed leaflets, upper-class women met to protest,
and more humble women joined the protests with their husbands. They
boycotted British goods, furnished food and supplies to militants, and
helped to sabotage British interests. A small number even lost their
lives: in April 1919 a twenty-eight year old widow was killed when the
British fired into a crowd, and at least four other women were counted
among the dead in later clashes with the occupation forces.[42]

Photographers sent to cover the nationalist demonstrations of 1919
shot carriage-loads of veiled women holding anti-British signs and participating in marches, speeches, and protests. The West and the Western press had an interest in the Egyptian revolution because of the
country's strategic location at the crossroads of Asia and Africa, and

because the Suez Canal played a critical part in Britain's imperial strategy in India.[43]

When the revolution stirred hope that the Wafd would soon win independence from the British, a thousand women met in St. Mark's Church in Cairo in January 1920 to form the Women's Central Committee of the Wafd party. This committee played a prominent role in the movement to boycott British goods in 1922, fully expecting that in return the party would support women's rights. At its founding meeting Huda Shaarawi (1879–1947) was elected president, and for a time women had an official structure from which to conduct nationalist activities.

In 1922 Great Britain granted Egypt partial independence and the following year the Egyptians established a new constitution. Gender was not mentioned in it. Articles 74 and 83 at first seemed to grant universal suffrage in electing members to the Senate and the Chamber of Deputies but a subsequent amendment restricted suffrage and office-holding to men. The women who had been so active were profoundly disappointed.[44] Neither classical liberalism nor democratic practice extended to half the Egyptian population in this period. Women were denied full and equal membership in the community and deprived of the most basic freedoms available to male citizens.[45] Huda Shaarawi later wrote in her memoirs:

> Exceptional women appear at certain moments in history. . . .
> They rise in times of trouble when the wills of men are tried. In
> moments of danger, when women emerge by their side, men utter
> no protest. Yet women's great acts and endless sacrifices do not
> change men's views of women. Through their arrogance, men
> refuse to see the capabilities of women. . . .
> Women reflected on how they might elevate their status and
> worth in the eyes of men. They decided that the path lay in participating with men in public affairs. When they saw the way
> blocked, women rose up to demand their liberation, claiming their
> social, economic and political rights. Their leap forward was greeted with ridicule and blame, but that did not weaken their resolve.[46]

Despite the defeat, however, women were undeterred. Nabawiyya Musa, Huda Shaarawi, and others organized the Egyptian Feminist

Union in 1923 and adopted a strategy akin to the one used by non-governmental organizations (NGOs) today carving out a territory in which it could operate.

Upper-class activists mobilized like-minded women to weaken misogynist local culture and turn subjugated women into energetic citizens. In contrast to Egyptian male reformers who sought to emulate the advances made in European society, Egyptian feminists never tried to replicate the experiences of Western women. Although they appreciated the advances of feminists abroad and were mindful of the developments in the international feminist arena, they focused narrowly on their own concerns.

Upper-class women again appealed to the nation's leaders for suffrage, educational rights, and employment opportunities. In public meetings, newspaper articles, and private discussions they urged government officials to establish a social welfare system that would provide health care and child rearing for poor people. They pressed for legal reform of the personal status law.[47] While the EFU did not achieve what it set out to do, it at least planted the idea that the state had a responsibility to provide for the health, education, and economic well being of the masses.[48]

Huda Shaarawi's privileged social background, stemming from her wealthy father and well-connected and affluent husband, provided her protection from critics and gave her a platform from which to speak on controversial gender issues. Shaarawi was raised in Cairo and belonged to the last generation of women to reach maturity while the harem system still prevailed. Her father was a rich landowner who died when she was five years old and her mother was a former concubine. At the age of twelve Shaarawi was promised in marriage to her cousin and legal guardian, 'Ali Shaarawi, an economic alliance designed to ensure that Huda's father's land and wealth would be kept in the family. Custom required that she leave her family and go to live with her husband's household when she turned thirteen. The union proved unhappy for the young bride because 'Ali Shaarawi was already married and unwilling to divorce his first wife. Unable to tolerate married life, Huda returned to her family home when she was fourteen and remained there until she was twenty-one years old. Under duress she then returned to her husband and bore him two children.

Huda became an active philanthropist and established a number of organizations to aid poor women and children. As charitable activities were broadened after the 1919 revolution, Huda joined a group of privileged women who reached out to the needy, in the process gaining organizational and managerial skills and carving out for themselves public space in which they could respectably function.

After her husband's death in 1922, Huda Shaarawi devoted herself to the Egyptian Feminist Union, serving as president until 1947; she also helped found and, from 1945 to 1947, acted as president of the Arab Feminist Union. She founded newspapers, participated in international women's activities, and gave lectures at conferences in Egypt, the Arab countries, Turkey, and Europe.[49] Huda became the symbol of Egyptian feminism, not the least for one of her earliest and most radical acts, the public removal of her veil, which she did returning from a conference of the International Woman Suffrage Alliance in Rome as a delegate of the EFU. She and her trusted associate Saiza Nabarawi (1897–1985) both removed their veils at the Cairo train station. Shaarawi and Nabarawi risked family censure, punishment, and humiliation for defying male privilege. Although conservatives criticized this gesture, it was not a crime, so they could not be punished by the state. Since Shaarawi was the widow of a prominent and influential Wafdist party leader, her defiance of convention had to be overlooked.

Upper-class women in the postindependence period hoped that lifting the veil would produce symbolic as well as practical results, and they were poised to take advantage of the removal of rigid gender prohibitions in society.[50] From the very beginning of the constitutional period, however, they suffered setback upon disappointment. They were denied the vote and excluded from the opening of the first parliament in 1924 (unless they were wives of ministers and other officials). In protest, members of the Egyptian Feminist Union and the Wafdist Women's Central Committee picketed the event, objecting to their exclusion from public life and challenging the idea that women's political activism was permitted only during moments of national crisis, such as during the Egyptian revolution, when extraordinary emergency measures were necessary. Male leaders, however, refused to sanction a redefinition of women's roles and were unwilling to grant women equal citizenship rights. Women were no longer needed, and they were expected to return home to care for their husbands and children.[51] But feminist women were no longer passive. Saiza Nabarawi, an ardent feminist, peace activist, journalist, lecturer, and editor in chief of the feminist journal *L'Egyptienne*, tried to enter Parliament in 1925 when the third session was held. Prevented from entering because of her gender, she wrote a stinging article she headed "Double Standard."

> Last Monday . . . was the . . . day of the third convocation of parliament. . . .
>
> Like many others, I dared to make one timid request. But what was I in this ocean of assembled greats! Wife of a minister? Wife of an ambassador? I am far from having this importance. . . .
>
> I had thought that my new position as editor-in-chief of *L'Egyptienne* would allow me to pass among the invited officialdom. . . . But, what after all is *L'Egyptienne* but a humble monthly magazine which has none of the privileges of a newspaper! This is the least of what the Minister of the Interior told me. . . .
>
> Allowing my humble person into such an honourable assembly would signal that the state was honouring Egyptian women and Egyptian men equally. . . . The Egyptian woman who constitutes half the nation was therefore totally forgotten. . . .
>
> Is it just that in this Egyptian land . . . our women should be the last to enjoy the rights and prerogatives accorded others, and that this should happen under a [Liberal Constitutional] ministry which proclaimed . . . that through higher education it hopes "to place men and women on an equal footing in order to permit the latter to fulfil their duty in the national renaissance"?[52]

Although members of the EFU argued that the denial of civil and political rights to women represented an injustice, the male political elite had asserted its authority. This decision to proscribe women from performing the duties of citizenship was consistent with the traditional power men possessed: men assigned social roles and women accepted their designated lot. The assumption that women belonged at home corresponded with the view that because women symbolized the self-identity of the nation, its spiritual essence, and its cultural integrity, they needed to remain with the family. The patriarchal family survived because the state circumscribed the temporal rights of women and allowed Muslim religious authorities exclusive administration of personal status laws.

At this time Egyptian feminists did want to change social relations in society, but they were not radical firebrands whose intention was to tear down religion or the family. Endorsing a moderate to conservative view of the family, they accepted the traditional sexual division of labor and respected Islamic dictates on the roles women and men should play. In Margot Badran's view, what women desired was equality in difference rather than the reciprocity of rights and responsibilities.[53]

The EFU became their principal vehicle; its membership had reached two hundred and fifty women by 1929.[54] Members set up a school and health clinics in the province of Minya, an undeveloped region in southern Egypt, and a model farm in Giza, located on the outskirts of Cairo, in the mid-1930s. They hosted the Conference for the Defense of Palestine in 1938 as a gesture of solidarity with Palestinian women fighting the expropriation of Arab land by incoming settlers. They held the first Pan-Arab Feminist Conference in 1944, which resulted in the establishment of the Arab Feminist Union.[55]

During this first phase social homogeneity and ideological cohesion characterized the feminist community, although by the late 1930s the EFU was beginning to break down into factions. Newer members protested the group's disinclination to recruit a more socially diverse membership. The upper-class women of the organization, whose worldview was largely secular and foreign, spoke French, wore Western dress, and looked to Europe for their cultural enrichment. Challenging them were the more recently organized middle-class women who spoke Arabic and were rooted in local culture and traditions. They disapproved of the upper-class-based character of the movement and the goals of Egyptian feminism.

World War II altered the political landscape in Egypt and contributed to the growth of Islamic fundamentalism, communism, and a more broad-based feminism. It also spawned a nationalist resurgence. As more radical ideologies gained ground, liberalism and its practitioners were put on the defensive. The political discourse in the country became more strident and more oppositional, and the EFU found itself under attack from within. While class-based tensions could not be avoided, ideological differences also produced dissension and the withdrawal of members from the group.

The experiences of Zainab al-Ghazali, while not typical, did suggest that there were strains in the movement. As a young woman in the mid-1930s, al-Ghazali joined the Egyptian Feminist Union. But after she took a religious seminar at al-Azhar University she became devout in her religion and finding the secularism of the EFU objectionable she left the group and founded the Muslim Women's Society.

Women like Duriya Shafiq (1908–1975), Inge Aflatun (1924–1989), and Latifa al-Zayat (b. 1924), at the other extreme, embraced more radical ideas and were prepared to engage in more aggressive strategies for change. Their tactics were populist, their goals comprehensive, and their tone forceful. In this era of feminist politics new organizations and dynamic younger leaders demanded that women gain the right to vote and made social critiques of the economic system that, in their view, caused the subordination of women.[56]

Among the new associations that were founded was the Egyptian Feminist Party, established by Fatma Nimat Rashid in 1944; it was the first exclusively political women's party. Its platform supported social and economic reforms, and it was the first feminist group to advocate birth control and abortion. Rashid's position on abortion, considered very radical at the time, was rejected by Islamic clerics. The ulema were outspoken in their opposition to the practice, although, unlike Catholics, Muslims believe that life begins only at the time of "quickening" or at the moment when a mother feels life in her body.[57]

Membership in the Egyptian Feminist Party was spare and consisted mainly of middle-class professionals, with writers, journalists, and teachers predominating. Despite its earnest platform, the group's numerical weakness made it politically ineffectual.[58]

Another feminist, Duriya Shafiq, founded an organization called Bint al-Nil (Daughter of the Nile) in 1948, with some other educated middle-class women. Shafiq was born in the Egyptian Delta town of Tanta, where she received a French education in religious missionary schools.[59] After matriculating at the Sorbonne, she wrote a doctoral dissertation on "La Femme Egyptienne et l'Islam." She then returned to Egypt to look for a position. She was denied a teaching job at Cairo University apparently because the dean would not assume the responsibility of hiring such a "beautiful woman" for his staff. She then accepted a position with the Ministry of Education, but administrative work proved unsatisfying, so she left this job and became a journalist; she founded three women's magazines.

Bint al-Nil campaigned for female suffrage, representation in Parliament, and equal political rights. Arguing that the constitution of 1923 guaranteed the equality of the sexes, she became a tireless advocate of the franchise for women and the election of women to political office. She also supported an agenda of social reform, emphasizing the importance of health and social services, literacy, and job creation for poor women. Through provincial branches of the organization its members offered literacy and health classes to the indigent. Shafiq believed that women were entitled to an identity outside the boundaries of home and marriage and favored changes in personal status laws in an effort to improve women's status in the family.

One of Shafiq's articles in the newspaper *Al-Misri* (May 1952) captures her spirit and demonstrates her determination.

> Let the enemies of women muster everything in their arsenal and let them imagine that they can stop the march of time and progress. They will never succeed, except in harming the reputation of their country and their tolerant and generous religion which when understood truly will not hinder the advancement of nations and the development of their people, men and women.

In 1952 Shafiq also submitted her registration papers in an attempt to run for a seat in Parliament. It was, of course, rejected, because women had no political or constitutional standing in the country. She filed suit before the State Council, asking that the election law be amended. While she was not successful, Shafiq made the point that citizenship should grant to men and women equal participation in the political system.[60]

Shafiq converted Bint al-Nil into a political party in 1953 just as Abd al-Nasir closed down all independent political organizations. Determined to continue her political activity, Shafiq participated in demonstrations calling for women's right to vote, wrote newspaper articles, and delivered lectures. She also undertook hunger strikes with colleagues and supporters on behalf of those causes.

In addition to Fatma Nimat Rashid and Duriya Shafiq, whose activity derived from the foundation set by the Egyptian Feminist Union, a new breed of leftist feminists also emerged from the communist underground. Although the Egyptian communist movement was largely male in membership, women became involved in small numbers. Devoting themselves to radical politics, young middle- and upper-class women rejected the social conservatism of the family and the class-bound rigidity of society. Applying a class analysis to gender relations, they condemned the quasi-feudal social relations of the past as well as the nascent capitalist conditions of the present. In rejecting arranged marriages and protesting women's limited experience with education, business, and professional life, they held government and religious officials responsible for the second-class status of women in society. Within the cosmopolitan world of leftist politics, in the lycée and in the university, men and women mingled together socially and academically. In this narrow world of radical politics gender barriers broke down to an extent and traditional roles were challenged.

While modern emancipated women were a small minority in the middle and latter 1940s, they did exist, and some went on to become leaders of the students', women's, and leftist movements. For example, Inge Aflatun was a Marxist, feminist, and gifted artist. Latifa al-Zayat, who was a student leader in the university and involved in radical politics, later became a writer and novelist. Inge Aflatun described her background and her introduction to leftist politics:

> I was born in Cairo, into a family of large landowners. . . . The family spoke French which was typical of bourgeois families at the time. . . . My introduction to politics came through the social and economic conditions of the time. I was shocked by the poverty and by the differences between classes. . . . The dissatisfaction I felt was present in my first paintings. . . . At the lycée, I met people, discussed things, found Marxist books, was in contact with young Egyptian intellectuals. Then I became a Marxist.[61]

Inge Aflatun's childhood was atypical in many ways, but, in particular, her mother offered her an alternative view of women's place in society. Aflatun watched her mother become an independent working women—indeed, a modern role model. In the 1930s women who engaged in self-directed professional economic activity were rare in Egypt. Few women had either the personal ambition, necessary start-up capital, or support of their families to establish their own businesses. Almost none were considered worthy credit risks by local banks to be granted loans. Yet, in 1936, Inge Aflatun's mother rejected tradition and opened a fashion boutique in Cairo, after receiving a loan from Bank Misr. This required considerable courage since her husband strongly discouraged her entrepreneurial efforts. He even attempted to insulate his two daughters from their mother's example by enrolling them in a Catholic school whose mission was to educate girls to obey their husbands and accept their traditional place in society. In her memoirs Inge recalls that her father insisted on having his daughters attend this school so they would not grow up like their mother.[62]

Another activist, Latifa al-Zayat, recollected her communist beginnings:

> I was born in a small town overlooking the Mediterranean, Damietta, in 1924 . . . into a lower middle class or upper petty bourgeois family . . . and I came to Cairo in 1936 for my education. I began university in 1942–1943 . . . . By the time I was in university, I lost all hope in the existing parties because they failed to answer the national question. I became a Marxist or a communist from a nationalist point of view. What appealed to me very much in Marxism . . . was the ethics . . . the absence of discrimination in religion, race, sex.[63]

Leftist feminist women of the 1940s did not work with existing women's organizations largely because the ideological differences were too basic to overcome. Having become increasingly sensitive to the problems affecting poor women in Egypt, they extended themselves to working-class women in factories, focusing on the national question generally, and on social issues relating to health, education, and the family. Representatives of the movement also attended international conferences in an effort to familiarize others with Egyptian society.

Leftist women set up a new group in 1944–45 called the League of Women Students and Graduates from the University and Egyptian Institutes. The league attracted some fifty women, among whom were Inge Aflatun, Fatma Zaki, Latifa al-Zayat, and Soraya Adham. Adopting progressive views about women's role in society, the league called for the right of women to vote, the responsibility of the state to set up children's nurseries and guarantee social insurance and security, equal pay for equal work, and democracy. Although a number of the league's members became active communists, the group did not plan to recruit women into the underground movement. Instead, it conceived of itself essentially as a gathering place for young women who were interested in both the gender-oriented problems of women and the larger difficulties challenging Egypt as a nation—in particular, the struggle against British colonialism.

A pamphlet published by the organization instructed women to "struggle to create a free, noble life for Egyptian women under the sovereignty of a free and noble country; struggle to realize democratic freedom which cannot arrive under the shadow of the imperialist and imperialism nor under the shadow of enslavement and exploitation."[64]

During the league's existence the First World Congress of Women, organized by the Féderation Démocratique International des Femmes, was held in Paris in November of 1945. The league sent Inge Aflatun, Suad Kamil, and Safiyya Fadl as its representatives. Inge Aflatun described her experience:

> All of what we saw there left a great impression. I made a very powerful speech in which I linked the oppression of women in Egypt to the British occupation and imperialism. I not only denounced the British, but the King and the politicians as well. . . . I called for national liberation and the liberation of women. My ideas were applauded.[65]

The events prompted Aflatun to write her first book, *Eighty Million Women Are with Us*, which was published in 1948. The league, however, was never able to contribute significantly to the improvement of gender relations in Egypt or to broad political struggle since it existed for only a short time. It was closed by the government in 1946, along with some dozen groups considered politically hostile, in a campaign to eliminate suspected opposition to the regime.

The mid- and latter 1940s were also a heady time for student activism, and women such as Enayet Adham, Latifa al-Zayat, Fatma Zaki, and Soraya Adham became leaders in the movement. In particular, Latifa al-Zayat was admired for her spirit and courage. She was said to electrify her peers with her dynamism and zeal whenever she addressed a university audience.[66] In recognition of her talents she was elected to the Committee of Students, which became part of the National Committee of Workers and Students. While this group did not constitute a disciplined political opposition, its protests against the occupation and the government in the mid-1940s attested to the deep distress of the population.

Al-Zayat's central role in university politics was not completely accepted. She noted, "I fought against the Muslim Brotherhood which tried to defame my reputation—they called me a prostitute and other such things. I remember I went home and wept. But I said, 'This is public work, this is not the last time I will be defamed.' "[67]

The women who entered the world of oppositional politics did so while they were students or after graduation, or they were the wives and sisters of men already involved. Although they were grappling with the issues of national independence and women's liberation, leftist women directed most of their efforts toward the general political front where they thought the greatest progress could be achieved. Most leftist women shared the view of Latifa al-Zayat. She remarked:

> It is a luxury to think of the liberation of women . . . when you see your brothers, fathers, and children strangled, scorned, and exploited by foreigners and local men and women. It is only when civilization reaches a certain level that the problems of women, children, and minorities become urgent. Women make the most noble contribution to the liberation of society when they embrace causes outside themselves and outside their families. . . . Women's fight for liberation implies a fight for the liberation of society.[68]

Leftist women endorsed the view that the nationalist struggle should take precedence over feminist issues. In addition to their work in the underground, communist women also engaged in legal nationalist activity. Along with noncommunists they joined the peace movement, which gained momentum in the early 1950s, and founded the Women's Committee for Popular Resistance in 1951 to support the fighting that had broken out against the British in the Suez Canal zone. Rather than blending nationalist, socialist, and feminist politics and attributing equal importance to each, they accepted the male view that the nationalist struggle was the core battle to wage. Although gender equality was not resolved within the communist movement, leftist women were active politically and hopeful that their contributions would mean a better life for men and women.

The Debate Over Personal Status Law

Upper- and middle-class women began to push back the boundaries of seclusion through their voluntary social service activities, their nationalist and feminist campaigns, and their support for the state's expansion of educational opportunities for girls. In contrast to the aforementioned changes in the public arena, the patriarchal structure of the family remained fully intact. Because state officials were reluctant to alienate conservative social forces while in the embryonic stages of nation building, they were prepared to maintain traditional social relations in the family. In return for participation in the newly created liberal constitutional state, lawmakers yielded to secular and religious conservatives who would never countenance revision of traditional family life.[69]

Gender relations in the family were sustained through the maintenance of personal status codes, or laws, relating to marriage, divorce, child custody, guardianship, and inheritance. Deriving from Islamic or Sharia law, the personal status laws defined women as legal subordinates to men. According to the Hanafi school of Sharia law that is observed in Egypt, a husband is charged with the responsibility of supporting his wife and children financially, and in return he is authorized to restrict his wife's movements, confine her activities, and make decisions on her behalf. A wife, who is obliged to care for her spouse and children, must obey her husband.

Personal status codes were not simply traditions sanctioned over the centuries. They were laws in place during the liberal age, and they remain in place, with modest variations, today. The codes are important because men utilize them to validate their domination over women. Citing the applicability and immutability of Islam, they impose their will and shape the character of the family. As a result, instead of allowing women to take their legitimate place as citizens of the nation-state, men have kept women separated from one another and divorced from the business of the country. Women's lives have been bifurcated into two dichotomous parts, split between their tenuous role as members of the nation-state and their more accepted family position as mothers and wives.

Personal status laws reflect and define the patriarchal structure of the society and institutionalize inequality within the family.[70] Huda Shaarawi and Duriya Shafiq fought continuous battles to change family law provisions, and Shafiq even debated shaykhs from al-Azhar on the subjects of divorce and polygyny. But such feminist efforts were largely ignored.

Even committees set up by the state itself, such as those in 1920 and 1929, whose intent was to institute moderate reforms in Islamic family law, accomplished little because secular politicians were reluctant to intervene in the private domain of the family. Their hesitation allowed personal status laws exemption from temporal regulation. As a result, polygyny continued to be in force during the liberal age and divorce remained the prerogative of the husband. In fact, a man was not even required to defend his position in a court of law. In contrast, a woman seeking divorce was compelled to meet strict conditions by proving either lack of male economic support or serious male illness. While other sections of the legal system such as commercial, financial, criminal, and penal law became secularized, the arena of personal status remained largely unchanged.[71]

In the end, the liberal state improved education and employment opportunities for small numbers of Egyptian women and girls and liberalized, to a modest extent, women's participation in public life. However, it maintained Islamic family law, allowing men almost total control over women.[72] Women were denied social and political agency and access to the institutions of power. Hisham Sharabi identifies this as the dominant ideology of neopatriarchal society: a male-oriented philosophy that assigns privilege and power to men at the expense of women. Even though liberalism allowed the most socially prominent women the space to organize politically, publish their views, and carry out social welfare projects, the vast majority of women were crippled by the economic, legal, and social constraints placed upon them.[73] Without the vote, lacking representation in Parliament, and deprived of access to the main sources of power, women ultimately had no authority to change social, legal, and political life in the country.

CHAPTER THREE | Women and the State
During the Nasir Years

THE LIBERAL DEMOCRATIC SYSTEM IN place since World War I collapsed in July of 1952 when a small, clandestine, politically diverse group of low-level military officers carried out a coup d'état against a government they regarded as corrupt and too weak to win independence from the British, allow political representation, or achieve economic development. The revolutionaries were organized as a secret oppositional movement within the military and had supporters in most of the political factions in Egypt, including the communists, Islamists, and nationalists. Having established close bonds as military cadets, they cemented their relations through common service experience, army discipline, and combat. Despite their sometimes conflicting and incompatible ideologies, they rallied behind the revolutionary leadership of Gamal Abd al-Nasir and supported at least some of his policies: abolition of the monarchy, restriction of the power of the landlords, industrial development, international realignment, and, most important, realization of full Egyptian independence from Britain. The coup overthrew the king and replaced the liberal state with a closed and politically rigid system of military government. The military opposed democratic practice it regarded as too divisive, Western-oriented, and responsible for the country's underdeveloped state. The Nasirists crushed an upper-class elite that had until then wielded social, economic, and political authority. Egypt imported liberalism into the country but did not yet have an institutionalized civil society. Liberalism had not taken hold because

Egyptians were not culturally predisposed toward freedom of the individual as the paramount value.[1]

Over time the military government nationalized the Suez Canal, built the Aswan Dam on the Upper Nile River, introduced land reform designed to destroy the power of the landlords, nationalized the economy, and established a form of socialism in the country. The state became a strong advocate for industrialization with public investment in heavy industry, free education, and social welfare. Though the regime's pledge to create a modern, just, and prosperous society was not achieved, its commitment to improving the lives of the people was deeper than the liberal capitalist regime that preceded it.

During the Nasirist years Egypt experienced intellectual rigidity, international isolation, and economic stagnation. The agricultural sector languished and cities grew at an alarming rate as large numbers of rural migrants created or settled into already existing urban slums. In the urban sector the informal economic sector grew extensively. The military leaders resumed a battle that had been fought earlier by Muslim nationalists. In this crusade Enlightenment philosophy was condemned, individualism discredited, and Western humanism rejected as foreign. The masses of people, while outwardly supportive of the regime, remained largely apolitical, dashing any hopes to create a workable political structure that could serve the majority of the population.[2]

While Nasir was first and foremost a nationalist, he came to embrace the concept of pan-Arabism and adopted the theory of positive neutralism articulated by Tito and other allies. His close relations with the Soviet Union and the socialist bloc countries reflected his deep distrust of and alienation from the United States and Western European countries.

In keeping with military tradition and philosophy, there were no feminist-inspired issues on the revolutionary agenda of the Free Officers when they came to power.[3] Some of the goals of the women's movement were, however, in time appropriated by the Nasirist regime as part of its effort to modernize society. Women were given the vote and offered greater educational and employment opportunities. In retrospect, some regard Nasir's regime as a golden era for women's rights. The category of citizenship changed in this period to include women's suffrage and women's involvement in the nationalist struggle for modernization and development. He legitimized women's working outside the home for wages, marking a dramatic shift in the role of women in the formal economy. Many more girls and women attended schools and university as a result of free public education. Through Nasir's official parties women were encouraged to become involved in political life. As a result, women from diverse socioeconomic backgrounds became part of the process for modernizing the country.

The revolutionaries were political radicals but in ideologically varied ways; as a group they were socially conservative. In particular, they had no interest in extending their progressive attitudes to the private domain of the family, considering traditional domestic relations inviolable. Nasir left untouched laws governing marriage, divorce, and personal status. Women's rights to full citizenship were restricted because of the patriarchal construction of family life, which determined that women had no independent status once they married and were subordinated to the personal power of the husbands. Women's lives in the family structure remained unreformed.

Feminists were neither brought into decision-making positions nor consulted about the needs of female constituents. Since women did not serve in the military, they were not part of the revolutionaries' inner circle. Men continued to reserve for themselves the exclusive right to construct the categories of social and political behavior. This was not something the officers thought about consciously; rather, it was simply the "natural" course of action. As a result, gender-specific objectives remained outside the core of revolutionary ideology. In trying to alter Egyptian society military leaders focused on broadly achievable national goals that dealt primarily with changes in the structure of economic relations and political realignment.

The gains women did achieve were thought of by the regime not as the granting of civil rights but as a means of achieving economic modernization and nation building. The regime's strategy focused on classic issues of development, not on gender equity, and although legislation allowed women an increased public role in politics, education, and the economy, they were still expected to fulfill their traditional familial duties as prescribed by the Sharia.

Conventional family life was preserved and gender relations at home remained virtually unchallenged despite formal political equality for women and their entitlement to public sector jobs. Women worked outside the home for wages but still performed the conventional female tasks of child care and housekeeping. Although women's participation in the labor market increased, at least for younger and better educated women, and produced a degree of economic independence, economic change did not result in social or psychological emancipation for women as a broad group. Even though more women contributed to the family's income, they did not have a greater say in decision making. Because the regime was not prepared to connect reforms in the public domain with changes in the structure of home life, traditional definitions of gender were reformulated but not abandoned. The new leaders undermined the old forms of sexual segregation but at the same time denounced the noblesse oblige feminism of the previous era and retained a conventional gender-based framework in society.[4]

Because family relations were not recast, social exploitation carried on. As Bina Agarwal has argued in another context, the ideology of gender—especially the assumption that women are housewives and mothers and only secondarily workers and public figures—permeated policy and contributed to women's social and material inequality. The state, the media, and religious institutions implicitly accepted the superiority of men and could, therefore, justify women's unequal access to technology, credit, training, and resources.[5] Even though women were granted new rights as citizens, their primary identity during the socialist era remained in attachment to the family.

Public Advances for Women During the Early Socialist Era

Nasir's rise to power meant that for the first time in centuries native Egyptians ruled the country. The Turco-Circassian elite that had run the nation was superseded by native-born Egyptians and the ethnic minorities who had dominated business and professional circles lost their economic predominance to local Muslims and Coptic Christians. Egyptians now controlled the country's political, ideological, legal, and economic life, handled its cultural production, and regulated its administrative policies.

In the early years the new regime focused its domestic attention on consolidating power, winning independence from Great Britain, and initiating the process of modernization. By the summer of 1954 the liberal-age constitution had been abrogated, the monarchy overturned, political parties and organizations forbidden, and Nasir's vision of sin-

gle-party government established. Firmly in power, Nasir became the
only important actor in Egypt and the ideology of nationalism became
more radical. Because of his populist efforts to redistribute wealth
through land reform and state control of the economy, Nasir had the
support of the lower and middle classes.[6] In spite of the militarist control, new ideas surfaced and profound changes occurred, inspiring
guarded confidence among activists and nationalists alike. Feminists
like Duriya Shafiq, who were working to achieve political equality,
raised the now familiar argument that feminism complimented nationalism and that women deserved their rightful place in the new society.

During the 1950s and 1960s the state passed laws that transformed
women's public lives. Women became citizens in their own right:
women were given the vote and the right to hold public office, they
participated in government-run political organizations, and they entered government employment. In exchange for their contributions to
the nation's development, the state delivered social services to women
in the areas of education, health care, and job training.

Despite demonstrable advances, sharp contradictions existed for
women in these years. The state constructed a modernized secular society on the foundation of a centrally planned economy and pro-
claimed important public advances for women. But reform was offset
by the regime's acceptance of traditional family life. While military
leaders were prepared to incorporate women's labor into their plans
for modernization and development and eager to extend educational
opportunities, they were not predisposed either to challenge prevailing
patriarchal views or alter male privilege in the private domain.[7]

The 1956 constitution did provide landmark suffrage rights to
women. The newly promulgated constitution declared that all Egyptians were equal before the law and that there would be no discrimination on account of gender, racial origin, language, or creed (rule 31).
It endorsed the fair treatment of all employees in terms of work hours,
wages, insurance benefits, and vacations (rule 53) and required equality of opportunity for all Egyptians (rule 8). The state also promised to
support women's efforts to reconcile public work with family obligations (rule 19).[8]

While the right to vote marked an unprecedented advance for
women, progress was tempered by social conservatism and political
authoritarianism. The framers of the constitution diluted the voting

statute's impact, stipulating that though men were required to register, it was optional for women. The traditional assumption that men would elect parliamentary leaders on behalf of their dependent wives and daughters endured. Meanwhile, the image of women continued to be based on their dependent and subordinate role in the family.[9]

The right to vote provided women a connection to public life unrelated to the institution of the family and separate from their status as wives and mothers. Yet most Egyptian women initially ignored the franchise, apparently still viewing themselves as political appendages of their husbands. The statistics confirm that voting was perceived as a male activity and that female voting progressed slowly and incrementally. While over 5.5 million men had registered to vote in 1957, only 144,000 women chose to sign up. Women's registration reached 250,000 by 1965; by 1967 it had climbed to 1 million. In that same year only 11.5 percent of the male population had failed to vote, but a vast 76.7 percent of females abstained from exercising this right.[10] Conventional social attitudes coupled with Nasir's authoritarian style of government obscured the benefits of an active citizenry and complicated the process of turning passive women into vigorous civic participants. Women like Saiza Nabarawi, who had worked closely with Huda Shaarawi in the Egyptian Feminist Union, tried to reverse the apolitical character of women's lives by organizing a committee dedicated to educating women about their new rights as citizens.[11] Their task was an onerous one.

Since the franchise was conditional and restricted, it could not be expected to alter the structure of political life or solve the "woman's question." In a militarized society like Egypt in the 1950s and 1960s, there was an inherent skepticism about the value of suffrage itself. Democrats asked how meaningful the vote would be in a political culture in which Nasir exerted authoritarian control and withheld political freedoms from virtually the entire citizenship. In particular, voters were proscribed from organizing independently. They were prohibited from articulating demands and agitating for legal changes that could have improved their status in society. No activity separate from that sanctioned by the state was tolerated.

Nevertheless, due to the provisions of the constitution, "high politics," within the bounds set by Nasir, were opened to women. When elections to the National Assembly were held in July 1957, two women, one from Cairo and the other from Alexandria, were among the successful candidates for office, which women across Egypt regarded as a major political and psychological victory.

Defeating male opponents in open elections, Rawya Attiya of Cairo, a former captain in a women's commando unit, and Amina Shoukry of Alexandria, a volunteer welfare worker associated with Huda Shaarawi in the Feminist Union, convinced voters that selecting female legislators was consonant with history and tradition. Rawya Attiya said: "I was met with resentment for being a woman. Yet I talked to them [the voters] and reminded them of the prophet's wives and families until they changed their opinions."[12] The most venerated of political institutions was now open to all Egyptians. Saiza Nabarawi, who as a journalist and observer had been excluded from the opening of Parliament thirty years earlier, was finally vindicated. This election proved that the critics who challenged women's ability to engage publicly and politically were wrong.

The regime's support was necessary for election of men or women to office, and women parliamentarians necessarily became allies of the leadership whose nomination and endorsement elevated their candidacy. Men and women prevailed at the polls not because their ideas appealed to voters but rather because the state boosted them to victory.[13]

Within Nasir's program of modernization education reform became a centerpiece. To improve literacy and as a way to provide young people training for prospective careers in the burgeoning public sector, the government instituted compulsory education for boys and girls through the primary level (six years of schooling) and made instruction free of charge at all stages. The benefits to girls were demonstrable: in 1953 primary school enrollment stood at 37.7 percent female; by 1960 the figure had swollen to 56 percent. To Nasir's credit, between 1953–54 and 1970–71 the number of girls enrolled at primary school had risen a dramatic 170 percent. Under his administration female enrollment in general secondary education increased by an astonishing 631 percent, raising by sevenfold the pool of women with high school diplomas qualified to enter university. In fact, the female population at the university level climbed sixfold from the early 1950s when women represented 7.5 percent of all university students to 40 percent by 1970–71.

Literacy for women jumped from 12.4 percent in 1960 to 16.2 percent in 1976, and while the statistics seem modest, literacy for men remained practically unchanged, moving only slightly from 32.6 percent to 33.2 percent. Young women in particular who took advantage of Nasir's educational reforms became their most direct beneficiaries. Not only did the literacy rates among girls and young women rise by impressive degrees, but they gained skills and acquired a measure of independence and self-confidence unavailable to their mothers and grandmothers. Directly as a result of their newly acquired expertise, many entered the labor market in clerical, teaching, and administrative posts.

During Nasir's tenure in office the teaching profession was feminized. In 1961–62 the percentage of female teachers was 98 percent at the nursery level, 39.1 percent at the primary school level, 19.8 percent at the preparatory level, and 17.8 percent at the secondary level. By 1971–72 the numbers of women teachers increased at the preschool level to 99.6 percent, at the primary school level to 53.1 percent, at the preparatory and secondary school levels to 29.4 percent, and overall to 26.7 percent.[14]

Clerical education, in particular, became very attractive to young women. Between 1953–54 and 1970–71 the number of women enrolled in this specialized education, most of whom came from lower-middle-class social origins, increased 1,750 percent. While the government provided various training opportunities and work experiences unavailable before this time, its emphasis on secretarial posts for women betrayed the traditional attitudes of the military leaders. Channeling women into teaching and clerical positions, the regime created a division of labor by gender, with categories suitable for men and others for women.

By guaranteeing male and female university graduates and holders of intermediate degrees jobs in the state bureaucracy, Nasir ensured their political support for the regime. But his philosophical and economic principles were broadly appealing to many of Egypt's youth: Nasir offered the young a place in the system and he secured, in return, their allegiance.

The educational reform and liberalized work policies did much to broaden men's and women's horizons, increase personal development, cement loyalty to the regime, and contribute to national renewal. But in the generally segregated labor market, in Egypt and in much of the world, men were typically employed in the industrial and construction arenas while women were concentrated in clerical and service occupations. Although there were exceptions to the practice, because of the feminization of clerical jobs, women became dependent on the state for employment.

Women's health services also improved significantly during the 1960s when the government forged a free public health care system. Women benefited from the maternity and infant care centers set up by the regime in both rural and urban areas. In the centers women received free pre- and postnatal care and medications were available to them at modest cost. In 1951–52 216 centers had been established nationally; by 1968–69 the number had climbed to 1,743. As a direct consequence, mortality rates among pregnant women dropped significantly in the decades between 1948 and 1969.[15]

Public Policy and Ideological Change Under Nasir

Between 1952 and 1956 government officials expanded the public sector branch of the economy both to supplement private investment and to finance projects too ambitious for local entrepreneurs. The regime also introduced key land reform measures designed to break the socioeconomic power of large landlords and to involve the state in managing agricultural activities. Nasir forged a new social contract with the people, promising socialist control over the economy, subsidized food, free education and health care, and extensive employment opportunities.[16]

After Nasir entered into an arms deal with Czechoslovakia (with the Czechs acting as a cover for the Soviet Union), recognized the Communist government in China, and moved increasingly leftward politically, the United States and Britain withdrew their promise to help build the Aswan Dam. The dam was important to Egypt because it would regulate the flow of water for irrigation and produce hydroelectric power necessary for Egypt's increased electricity needs. In reaction, Nasir nationalized the Suez Canal and then faced down England, France, and Israel in the Suez War of 1956. Fearful that the West intended to undermine his rule, Nasir turned to the Soviet Union for the financial backing needed to accomplish his development objectives. By moving ideologically closer to the Soviet bloc, Nasir shifted Egypt's political ties to both eastern and nonaligned countries. Nasir launched a highly visible campaign to Egyptianize the country's economic and social life after emerging victoriously from the Suez War. He appropriated the assets of British, French, and Belgium nationals, seized banks, trading companies, insurance companies, and utilities, and took over a number of large manufacturing firms. Nasir's nationalist economic strategy was fueled by the conviction that the capitalist policies of the liberal age hurt ordinary citizens who had a right to the benefits of state services.

In 1959 the regime promulgated progressive new labor laws that lessened structural gender discrimination in the workplace by guaranteeing legal rights and special protection to working women.[17] The labor code stipulated paid maternity leaves of up to fifty days during which time women received 70 percent of their wages, two half-hour breaks per working day for mothers of infants during the eighteen months following delivery without any deductions in pay, protection from dismissal during pregnancy and childbirth so long as absenteeism does not exceed six months, and day care facilities in establishments employing over one hundred women.[18] Nasir instituted remarkably progressive employee rights provisions, facilitating the entrance of mothers into the labor market. American society has yet to duplicate much of what Nasir achieved.

By 1963 women made up over 10 percent of the formal sector working population, and lower- and middle-class families came to depend upon the joint income of husbands and wives. Nasir's modernization strategy included women, but the regime made no effort to convince the population that women had the right to work outside the home. Consequently, the attitudes of older socially conservative men and women changed little.[19]

Entrepreneurs withheld investment in the economy, anticipating that their businesses would be nationalized by the state. This and the sagging financial condition of the early 1960s forced the government to take drastic economic measures. Through Nasir's "Arab socialism" the government nationalized large- and medium-scale industrial enterprises and centralized all economic activity. Trying to solve a number of problems simultaneously, Nasir created countless new jobs for both men and women in the burgeoning bureaucracy. His hope was to invigorate the economy, increase his circle of supporters, and demonstrate to local capitalists that socialist economic policies could effectively build the nation. In state offices and factories men and women

took up Nasir's call to participate in Egypt's renaissance. State employees, especially, became the beneficiaries of Nasir's policies, with
women workers experiencing improved health care, maternity leaves,
and child care services. With a greater number of females engaged in
paid employment in the early 1960s, cultural stereotypes were increasingly being confronted by younger men and women and some
were even beginning to renegotiate their relations in the workplace and
in the family.[20]

In 1962, the government promulgated the Charter for National Action, which offered a new paradigm for development in Egypt and
identified the state's strategy for regional development. The charter af-
firmed Nasir's ideology of revolution, socialism, and unity and endorsed women's equality as citizens. The authors of the charter wrote:

> Equal opportunity is the expression of social liberty, and it can
> be specified in some basic rights for every citizen which should
> be realized: First, every citizen has a right to medical care. . . .
> Secondly, every citizen has a right to education according to tal-
> ent. . . . Thirdly, every citizen has a right to work suitable to
> one's capabilities. . . .
>
> Woman must be made equal to man and she must therefore
> shed the remaining shackles that impede her free movement, so
> that she may play a constructive and profoundly important part
> in shaping the life of the country.
>
> Children are the makers of the future and it is the obligation
> of our working generation to provide them with all that is nec-
> essary to successfully carry out that responsibility.[21]

In this last passage the state did not specifically suggest that it was
a woman's duty to rear children; rather it referred to the responsibility of the working generation, presumptively denoting both men and
women.[22] The choice of these words is very significant; indeed, it car-
ries revolutionary implications. However, the government did not exercise its cultural hegemony and direct people to engage in a discussion
of social roles or gender equity. This is probably because the military
rulers had no intention of carrying out a social revolution or defying
the conservative forces whose cultural convictions held that women's
rightful place was inside the home serving their husbands and children.

The Charter for National Action again established its progressive agenda by approving, in principle, birth control and family planning—two highly controversial issues in Egypt. Aziza Hussein, a highly respected Egyptian diplomat and pioneering family planning advocate, argued in the early 1960s that an explosive population could be sustained neither economically nor politically. She was not alone in her alarm at the rising birthrate. The government, too, began to recognize the destabilizing effects of unplanned population growth. Natural increase coupled with uncontrolled rural migration to Cairo posed myriad problems. Not only did the city lack suitable and affordable housing, adequate employment opportunities, a sanitation infrastructure, and schools, but as less and less food was grown in the countryside, urban residents became potential agents of civil strife.[23] While in Western society birth control, abortion rights, and women's power to manage their bodies constitute the core of the feminist movement, during Nasir's regime the campaign in favor of family planning dovetailed with his economic agenda and did not have a consciously feminist dimension.

Aziza Hussein campaigned tirelessly for the wider spacing of pregnancies, the improvement of health care for mothers and their young, and better access to birth control information and devices. With support from the Pathfinder Fund, a nongovernmental organization working in the field of population control, the Cairo Women's Club, of which she was president, and the minister of social affairs (who was the only female cabinet member), Hussein brought family planning to Egypt. Remarkably, after only a few years work, twenty-two family planning clinics had been set up in the country, confirming women's interest in the information the centers offered. Capitalizing on this momentum, in 1966 the government promoted an official population program, followed a year later by the establishment of the Egyptian Family Planning Association under the aegis of the Ministry of Social Affairs. Because the regime appropriated this issue as its own, committing its resources and influence, Aziza Hussein withdrew her active involvement.

Aziza Hussein tried to interest women's club members, social welfare activists, and administration representatives in a discussion of Muslim family law, which she, like others before her, identified as a major source of women's subordination. She did not succeed. In the absence of an independent women's rights movement no organized challenge could be mounted on this issue, and the regime was unresponsive, reflecting its tendency not to tackle controversial social issues that might alienate social conservatives.

Nasir's regime prohibited political groups from functioning autonomously, but it made several attempts to create state-run mass organizations—the first in 1953 with the formation of the Liberation Rally and the second in 1957 with the establishment of the National Union. The military had intended that each would generate support for the regime and provide activists with a means to channel their energy. These groups were designed to demobilize the masses, to confine people's activities to very limited spheres. Unlike political parties, they did not encourage popular participation in the process of governing or involve members in the decision-making process. Both ventures, conceived simply as catalysts of support to the regime, failed to inspire popular allegiance.

The regime's third and most ambitious attempt to create a mass organization came in the early 1960s with the formation of the Arab Socialist Union (ASU). Units of the ASU were set up in schools, factories, cities, and towns with the goal of recruiting Egyptian workers, women, journalists, students, military men, and peasants. ASU organizers were nationalists who came mainly from the petite bourgeoisie. They were inspired by the prospects of radical economic policies, a new social order, and social justice for the popular classes. This was a constituency vital to Nasir and he granted it broad latitude to activate those who had been neglected by liberal-age politicians. The journalist and labor activist Amina Shafiq was among the generation of young adults who was predisposed to Nasir's nationalist-populist appeal. Because she benefited from the regime's commitment to educational reform, she was eager to reciprocate by participating in the new organization. She organized a literacy class for women in the Maaruf section of Cairo, distributed the newspaper of the Arab Socialist Union, and became engaged in the political discussions and debates.[24]

Like other idealistic men and women of the time, Amina Shafiq was caught up in the political momentum generated by the ASU and committed to improving Egypt's future. She and other nationalists who adopted a social justice perspective were hopeful that, once secure, the regime would permit democratic forces to emerge. But this was not to be.

Similar to the organizations before it, the ASU became an instrument of the regime. Abd al-Nasir and his lieutenants never allowed civil society to flourish because, despite the bases of support they established, they were dominated by the fear that political independence would lead to opposition and to their eventual ouster.

Though fundamentally secular in orientation, Nasir acknowledged the cultural and doctrinal significance of Islam. His tolerance of Islam was rewarded by the support of a new generation of Islamic modernists who provided a theological defense for the regime's policies. Religious moderates endorsed, for example, increased public activity for women in education, employment, and politics. In an influential work published in 1967, *The Koran and the Problems of Our Contemporary Life*, Ahmad Khalaf Allah argued that the Quran granted women political and economic rights. These privileges, which were honored during the Prophet's lifetime, were revoked by what the author called misguided successors. Defending the franchise and employment opportunities for women, he wrote that women were only requesting what was lawfully theirs.

Modernists sanctioned a woman's right to public space, stipulating that the Quran obliged women to contribute to the development of society. But like secular leaders of the regime, who advocated progressive public measures that transformed women's role in the economy and in the polity, modernists were disinclined to question the structure of the family or the patriarchal order of Islam.[25]

Women's identity was constructed by men in the ruling elite—in the legislature, the judiciary, and the religious establishment. Women's roles had been recast since the days of the liberal age, but in ways fitting to the new male leadership in society. In the socialist era women were citizens, more independent and publicly active than ever before. Yet, men continued to dominate the family and the workplace, and their authority was discernible in every sphere of life. Like the liberal age that preceded it, during Nasir's regime male dominance constituted a presumed aspect of male citizenship.

Mervat Hatem confirms this assessment and argues that while the state used feminist ideology to catalyze national and international support it was still patriarchal at its core. In addition to the all-male military leadership that monopolized the political arena, male bureaucrats dominated the public sector. While women were integrated into the

economy, they were situated at the lowest levels, with virtually no decision-making powers. Nasir appropriated a form of feminism, which
Hatem calls "state feminism," whereby he granted women economic
independence from their husbands or fathers but made them dependent on the state for social services such as education, health care, day
care, and employment. Since the private sector was structurally and
politically powerless, and unsympathetic to the advances of women,
the state became the sole engine of change. For Hatem, although
women benefited from its advances, state feminism or public patriarchy presupposed private patriarchy in the family and continued
women's dependency on men. In the end, women remained politically
weak and socially unequal.[26]

Yet, despite the limitations of the policies that Abd al-Nasir instituted and the Islamic modernists supported, a whole generation of
women felt that their public lives had changed. Women possessed the
vote, the right to work outside the home, and received the entitlements
of a social welfare system. The state succeeded in shaping their consciousness to the extent that many did not consider the connection between their active public roles and their traditional private duties. Arguably, the state's agenda was particularly subversive since it
reinforced women's private subjugation and made them complicitious
in their own inequality.[27] Women supported the state, embraced its ideology, participated in its modernization plans, and accepted their generally unreformed status in the family.

The state was successful in generating and solidifying support
among women because its spokesmen convinced them of its commitment to gender equity in the workplace, the school, and the political
organization. The regime's nationalist credentials, in addition, were
impeccable, and this held tremendous appeal. Contained within nationalist ideology was the presupposition that women had an economic and familial role to play in society's rejuvenation. While nationalism
made a place for women's rights, the breadth of change was limited.[28]
Nationalists argued that while the colonialist power had, in the past,
subdued the nation materially, it had never succeeded in extinguishing
the people's spiritual essence. That essence was to be found in the private arena of the family, which was seen as the domain of women. The
public/private dichotomy survived in the postindependence period;

women maintained their role in the home and men took charge of the public arena as their primary dominion.[29]

Notwithstanding the progress the regime achieved, its leaders suffered from a basic insecurity. Fearing repudiation, they allowed no room for dissent and undermined all independent political activity and nongovernmental initiatives. Inevitably, feminist organizations were demobilized and prohibited from organizing. When the regime crushed all autonomous political movements in 1954, feminist organizations, which had challenged patriarchal values, were outlawed. From this time forward, feminists could engage in the political arena only on Nasir's terms, terms that were fundamentally different from those envisaged by the activists themselves. As a result of the formulation of politics set in the early 1950s, activists had limited options available to them: they could either endorse the reforms the regime promulgated, remain silent with respect to their differences with the leadership, or be critical of the new structure and direction of society. In the highly charged political climate of the nationalist/socialist revolution, publicly defying the government was deemed domestically treacherous and could even be personally dangerous. When Nasir set up the authoritarian state, women worried that they would be forbidden to advance the campaign for women's rights.

Activist Women and the Nasir Regime

Less than a year after Duriya Shafiq had established the Bint al-Nil political party in 1953, that party and all other independent organizations were closed down by the authorities, who feared that autonomous civil activity might jeopardize the regime's efforts at consolidation and control. Without any institutional framework from which to organize and operate, feminists felt vulnerable to the immediate dislocations the revolution necessarily produced and were in a real sense disabled. Feminists, deprived of a structural base from which to lobby, were unable to influence policy. Not unexpectedly, when the Constitutional Assembly met in March 1954 it did so without female representation.

In protest, Shafiq and some fourteen to eighteen of her associates began a ten-day hunger strike in support of political rights and representation for women. A feminist hunger strike presented a distinctly new tactic in the struggle for women's equality and, carried out in the dawn of the new regime, it was a major embarrassment with explosive potential. Although women had typically been viewed as weak and dependent, these activists showed courage and strength and offered an example of direct action to other women. Muhammad Naguib, a national hero and the figurehead president of the country at the time, was given the job of diffusing the situation. Through Naguib's patient negotiation, with promises to convey Shafiq's views to the administration he represented, Nasir's surrogate managed to halt the protest.[30]

The state also deemed it necessary to dismantle the old Egyptian Feminist Union, allowing it to exist as a small social welfare society under the name of the Huda Shaarawi Association.[31] This produced a rupture in the organization. While some members supported the new regime in the hopes it would bring political and economic development to Egypt, Saiza Nabarawi was sharply critical of the authoritarian tendencies of the military leaders. Her dissenting view caused her to be ostracized by her comrades and barred from membership in the group. Saiza Nabarawi's activism would be tempered after her expulsion from the organization, an organization that she helped build and that played a central role in her life.

With coercive measures available to him, Nasir was able to expunge organized, independent feminist activity from the country. But, by the time his control over political life was firm, he came to understand that middle-class women strongly supported female suffrage. Not only activists in the mold of Duriya Shafiq and Saiza Nabarawi advocated for the franchise; moderate women such as the prominent journalist Amina al-Sayyid called for the vote. Al-Sayyid was the editor of *Hawa'* (Eve), a women's magazine, and a newly elected member of the reporters' syndicate—the professional association of journalists. In a public lecture she defended women's right to participate in the political life of the country, thereby preemptively dissenting from early reports indicating that the 1956 constitution would not grant suffrage to women. This single issue moved her from being an early supporter of Nasir's regime to being a critic. Early in the new regime the military authorities were sensitive to such sentiment and loathe to alienate potential supporters. Hence, the regime supported the vote for women, but explained in a memorandum accompanying the constitution that the law observed the principle of equality between men and women in registering to vote as part of its recognition of the important role played by women in public life for a long period of time and the manifest impact that this had on the development of the state. In view of the prevailing Egyptian customs, however, the registration of women to vote is left as a *choice* to be decided by each individual woman.[32]

In order to register, women were required to petition the state, a procedure that disadvantaged and intimidated illiterate women, whose direct contact with the government was ordinarily minimal. In contrast, middle-class women were generally untroubled by this disincentive since they possessed the self-confidence to approach government officials. As a result, the number of rural and poor urban women who exercised the franchise was disappointingly, but predictably, low. Thus, the campaign for women's rights seemed to take one step forward and another step backward.

Duriya Shafiq's political activities were partly responsible for women winning the vote. But she never worked with the regime. An unabashed critic of Nasir's policies, she deprecated the regime's commitment to social justice and even expressed nostalgia for the liberal democratic principles of the previous administration. Publically defying Nasir and the autocracy he headed, she called for the reinstatement of liberal-age policies. In the midst of revolutionary ideological and political ferment, her stance was anathema to the regime. Branded a bourgeois feminist and criticized for aligning with Western values and colonialist systems of government, she was silenced by a military establishment that could not tolerate her activism or countenance her opposition.

In 1957 Shafiq's public career as feminist, journalist, organizer, and nationalist was put to an end. Nasir prohibited her from participating in political action, closed down *Bint al-Nil* magazine, which she had founded in 1945, and banned her name from public print. She disappeared from political life after she was placed under house arrest in 1960. Remaining in near seclusion in her Cairo apartment for fifteen years, in 1975 her life ended when she fell to her death from her sixth-floor flat.

The results of Shafiq's political activity, like that of Inge Aflatun, Fatma Nimat Rashid, and Saiza Nabarawi, might be seen as indicative of the failed hopes of organized feminists: the government granted women the vote but simultaneously withdrew from them the right to organize politically. By way of example, when a diverse group of female activists tried to establish the National Feminist Union, they were denied a permit. Even when women mobilized during the invasion of the Suez Canal zone in 1956 and formed the Popular Resistance Committee, which gave women paramilitary and political training in support of the regime, military leaders stood fast against independent feminism. In the latter 1950s Shafiq was suppressed, Rashid's Feminist Party was dissolved, Nabarawi was muzzled, and Aflatun was imprisoned in 1959 for four years, along with hundreds of other communists.[33]

Aflatun stated in a series of interviews that when Nasir arrested female militants he consciously broke with a tradition that frowned upon the incarceration of women. The jailing of women (their number reaching thirty-five in the late 1950s and early 1960s) was apparently important to the regime because women's activities went beyond politics, to the very structure of society. Since women were still primarily identified as mothers, they could influence younger members of the family. In order to silence female critics of the regime and to protect the sanctity of the family, leftist women were arrested. Aflatun recalled women's experiences in prison:

> In prison we were initially cut off from the world: no books, no mail, no newspapers, no pen and paper. But the most difficult aspect was the rule against visits. . . . This was very difficult for the mothers among us. We made a very successful hunger strike—all of us—and they allowed us books, pen, paper, but still no visits.[34]

By denying women visits from their loved ones the regime intended to prevent them from politicizing family members and hoped to weaken their resolve. Leftist women connected feminism to nationalism and the class struggle, but since they operated underground in relatively weak organizations, and amidst significant state repression, their effect on society was limited.

Nasir recognized that the regime would be criticized for jailing mothers, so he forbade the press from publicizing the arrests. The tactic of secrecy, while typical of an authoritarian regime, was negated when the International Peace Committee learned of the lockup and disseminated the news inside Egypt and abroad.

In addition to the leftist women incarcerated, the regime sought to silence Islamic militants, of whom Zainab al-Ghazali was the most visible. Active before the 1952 revolution, al-Ghazali became highly prominent as head of the Muslim Women's Society after Nasir took power. Even though the Muslim Brotherhood was disbanded in 1953, the Muslim Women's Society continued to be officially recognized by the Ministry of Social Affairs. Al-Ghazali did not confine her activity only to women. In the late 1950s, along with an underground member of the Brotherhood, al-Ghazali worked clandestinely to revive the outlawed organization. Her activities did not go unnoticed by the regime, and in 1965 she was arrested and convicted of crimes against the state. Although the prosecutor demanded the death penalty, she was sentenced to twenty-five years in prison. During the nearly six years she served, she was continually humiliated by her jailers; some attempting to sexually abuse her. According to her own testimony, she defended herself in one attack by biting the neck of one of her attackers until he died.[35]

Nasir's regime began losing its credibility following the Six-Day War of 1967 and the devastating Egyptian loss to the Israelis. Right-wing and Islamic forces gained strength in the country and challenged Arab socialism, women's rights, and secular military authoritarianism. Nasir's opponents called for a return to Islamic values and cultural authenticity and the implementation of a new paradigm for economic and spiritual rejuvenation. The Islamist movement has steadily grown in strength and importance since the Nasir period and today is endorsed by considerable numbers of people in the middle and popular classes.

Women and the Nasirist State

Feminists have theorized about the state in different ways.[36] In the Marxist-feminist paradigm social reproduction, the family, and gender are analyzed in connection with the capitalist state, which is viewed as acting in the interests of the dominant class. The family is seen as institutionally reproducing labor power and maintaining existing social relations. Liberal feminists, in contrast, have drawn on the democratic views of Mill and Bentham and have argued that the state is a neutral force capable of advancing women's interests in society. While recognizing that men control state policies, they also believe that progressive legislation can promote equality in the state. For legal theorists such as Catherine MacKinnon the state is neither impartial nor virtuous. She argues that laws are patriarchal and the power structure is fraternal, with the result that male interests dominate. Women, as a group, are prejudiced by gender asymmetry and excluded from fully and equally participating in public life.

Catherine MacKinnon argues that the law treats women the way men see and behave toward women—adversely.[37] In her view, whether in public life—through language, religion, culture, politics, or the economy—or in the private domain of the family, law subjects women as a gender to the control of men. This analysis is applicable to the Nasir years. While nationalist men viewed women (and some women viewed themselves) as valued actors in the nationalist movement and as important contributors to the project of modernization, women continued to be treated as subordinates because the regime did not address personal status law or family relations. Although Nasir highlighted the state's legislative and practical advances in gender relations to demonstrate the regime's progressive philosophy, he did not challenge the conservative forces in society by attempting to recast the dynamic of family life.

Mai Ghoussoub has argued that the postcolonial regime of Abd al-Nasir was devoid of the kind of social critique advanced by the pioneers of women's liberation—Rifaa al-Tahtawi or Qasim Amin. Even though Nasirism promoted education, employment, and the franchise, women's position in society continued to be restricted by traditional social attitudes and by a military regime in which suffrage had relatively little meaning.[38] Women could not convert their right to vote into a powerful political force capable of changing laws, influencing policy, or acting with unified strength. That women's support was considered at all necessary to the regime reflected two assumptions: as socializers of the young, mothers could serve the government; as paid workers, women could contribute to building the new society. The regime expected women to instill in their families respect for authority and encourage adherence to administration policy. Its respect for the family, as required by religious law, was maintained while it mobilized half the population in the interests of nationalism and modernization. The government legitimized employment outside the home for women as a strategy to enhance state-run economic development and to enlarge the labor force. The Egyptian welfare state was set up to provide the economic basis of a new social contract between the Nasir regime and its key class allies, men and women of the middle class and labor aristocracy who were to staff the state sector.[39] The state advanced far beyond the liberal era by making a public commitment to equality for women. Through the provision of education, employment, health, child care, and other social benefits, it reduced the structural basis of gender inequality. To the extent that the regime was successful in communicating its modernizing ideas to women, it convinced sections of the urban female working population that it had been liberated by a forward-looking administration. But Nasir focused exclusively on political and economic advances; he was not attentive to the cultural world of Egyptians and did not believe he had license to enter the private domain of family life.

Although during Nasir's regime a limited number of women entered the previously male strongholds of the universities, the administration, the professions, industry, business, and politics, women were absent from the top levels of government, excluded from the judiciary and religious establishment, kept outside high-level business positions, and shut out of the military. Moreover, due to a combination of economic difficulties, high demographic growth, limited skills, and traditional attitudes, formal employment opportunities were still mostly restricted to middle- and lower-middle-class women, and the vast majority of working-class women were forced into the informal sector to find employment.[40] Legal citizenship was extended to women through the franchise. In return, women were expected to support the regime, advocate for it, and accept the conventional structure of family life.

Women did, however, feel empowered in a way that was new. Like the journalist Amina Shafiq, many women viewed themselves as contributing to revolutionary nationalist change and the making of a new society. This self-image stood in contrast to what the liberal age offered, when women had virtually no public rights. During the liberal era a wage earner was always a man, the breadwinner possessed an economically dependent wife at home who looked after his needs and those of the children, and a man's wage was viewed as the family wage.

In contrast, during the Nasir years women willingly became instruments of the regime and supported Nasir's mission because the state had convinced them that they performed important work in the society. In the area of employment women became engaged in a variety of positions, some connected with the home and some outside it—as dressmakers or cooks, midwives, agriculturalists, housewives, secretaries, factory workers, bureaucrats, or informal sector workers. Women's participation in the labor force increased by 31.1 percent from 1961 to 1969. While 43 percent of women worked in agriculture in 1961, the figure fell to 23 percent in 1969, with about half these women moving into the unconventional area of manufacturing. In fact, during these years the proportion of women working in the state manufacturing sector rose from 3.3 percent to 13.5 percent, not because the state was trying to neutralize the gender composition of the labor market but rather because additional hands were needed.[41] Moreover, since so few women were originally engaged in manufacturing, the actual number of women working in factories at this time was still low compared with other developing societies.

Women's employment as teachers, nurses, administrators and secretaries, and in public manufacturing was linked to an expansion of the state sector. In an extraordinarily progressive move, the state gave women wages equal to those being paid to men. This is an entitlement still absent in most societies today. Through its social service system it cautiously addressed the tensions involved in combining family life with paid employment.

Yet even during this most progressive era for women the majority of men still perceived women essentially as wives and mothers. Their wages were regarded as "supplementary" and male relatives continued to control their lives. While the civil right of women to work was acknowledged by the Nasirist state, it was not broadly internalized by men in the society. Outside the military government citizenship and work were two concepts men resisted applying to women.[42]

Women's paid employment may have empowered skilled and educated women from either the professional or the working classes and given them a measure of economic independence and autonomy, but the change did not alter social relations in general. Most women still remained socially inferior to men, and, because they were excluded from the military inner circle, they were responsible for few decisions affecting their public or private lives. Moreover, women's work at home was simply taken for granted; since it did not generate a wage it was not deemed important. Work, in conventional analysis, is only considered real for women when it interrupts the natural rhythm of the day and takes them away from the domestic labors where their main responsibilities are supposed to be centered. Andrea Rugh has observed that because the majority of women worked at home and did not receive a wage while most men labored outside the home for a salary, work was still synonymous with masculinity.[43] Fatna Sabbah supports this argument and has contended further that Muslim culture has a built-in ideological blindness to the economic dimension of women because women are perceived as sexual objects.[44] Moreover, it becomes easy to justify the unequal treatment of women in the workplace because women's most important identification is still linked to the family.[45]

In Egypt women were incorporated into the economic system as women rather than as workers. Gender, therefore, played an important role in how the workplace was structured, how relations in civil society were shaped, and how family life was organized. Carole Pateman has called men "unfree masters," by which she means that while some men are subordinate to their bosses as workers, men are always masters at home. In the institution of marriage men as husbands acquired a patriarchal right with respect to women as wives.[46]

Many women have been complicitous in maintaining this construction of gender relations by acting as stalwart defenders of a social order that views marriage and motherhood as key identifiers. The Egyptian short story writer, Alifa Rifaat, describes the emotional and cultural situation of a woman who had lost her spouse.[47] Her story is a common one.

> After [my husband] died I found myself in a different position. All my life I'd been ruled by a man, first my father and then my husband. I thought when he died I'd be free and on my own and would do as I liked. The trouble was though that I'd still got some life in me and was still young and I didn't find a hand stretched out to me as I struggled to bring you up. . . . At that time I felt that a woman without a man was like a fish out of water among people, and the women would look at her as a dan-

ger to their men and you'd find them keeping away from her as
though she were a dog with a mange.

For all its progressive legislation and action, the Nasir regime did not
carve out an independent space for women. Women's social identity as
well as self-identity reflected their attachment to the men in their lives.
If that connection was severed, the tenuous role of women in society
was made manifest.

Family life was constructed in such a way that men's control over
women in the private domain was legitimized. Herein lay the fundamental contradiction in society: state-sponsored "feminism" created a
new system of public gender relations while the old forms of private
patriarchy in the family were maintained.[48] Precisely because the government's reforms were inspired by patriarchal assumptions, they
could only have limited effect.[49]

CHAPTER FOUR | Gender Asymmetry During the Regimes of Anwar Sadat and Husni Mubarak

WHEN GAMAL ABD AL-NASIR DIED in 1970 he was officially succeeded by his vice president and longtime ally, Anwar Sadat. Sadat ruled through collective leadership for about the first eight months. Then leftist rivals who remained sympathetic to Nasir's socialist economic policies and his strategy of aligning internationally with third world and communist nations began to challenge Sadat's authority. He emerged victorious from the power struggle that followed and consolidated his power as the undisputed leader of Egypt. Once in control, he launched the so-called corrective revolution—a series of measures designed to distance himself from Nasir and the state-run policies he had fostered. Sadat dismantled the hated and feared internal security apparatus, expelled Russian advisers, encouraged Egyptian and foreign capitalists to invest in private industry, and reversed state control over the economy. In foreign policy, which became very important to Sadat both personally and politically, he established closer ties with the United States and other Western democracies and, before his death at the hands of a small group of Islamic fundamentalists in 1981, concluded a peace treaty with Israel that was a prelude to the return of the Sinai captured by Israel in the 1967 war.

During Sadat's tenure in office, he reversed Nasirism by eliminating the socialists from power, discrediting left-wing ideology, and liberalizing the economic and political systems. In a calculated action to weaken his Nasirist opponents, he released Islamic opposition members jailed by Nasir and undertook a strategic (but ultimately fatal) alliance with the religious opposition. As a centerpiece of his regime, Sadat introduced the controversial infitah policy, which involved encouraging foreign capitalists to invest in the country, seeking foreign aid, stimulating consumption, and strengthening the local bourgeoisie. Attempting to control the huge public sector while simultaneously stimulating private enterprise, Sadat hoped to launch broad economic change. Instead, his policies generated social and economic dislocation and political alienation. He lost support among the popular classes. The national debt increased, dependency on the West grew, and inequality between the social classes deepened. Egregious social problems intensified, characterized by a shortage of housing, unplanned expansion especially of Cairo, a rise in unemployment, and an upsurge in Coptic/Muslim tensions.

Bureaucratic inefficiency, debt, controversial foreign policies, and an absence of governmental credibility helped spawn a revival of traditional cultural "authenticity." For women, who had been the beneficiaries of improved education and job opportunities under Nasir, conflict surfaced as social conservatives rejected the Nasirist terms of women's citizenship and undertook to alter them.

As the public examined the "appropriate" place for women in society, two conflicting trends competed for women's attentions. Secularists approved women's participation in the marketplace, and in education, in opposition to Muslim fundamentalists, who articulated a restricted view of permissible behavior for women. At issue was, and is, women's place in the family, in wage labor, and in the public domain in general.

Toward the end of his life Sadat aggressively promoted women's rights. He instituted mandatory quotas for women in the electoral system and amended the personal status laws, two highly progressive actions. When Sadat authorized passage in the legislature of a modified personal status law granting women more control over marriage, divorce, and child custody, he was the first Egyptian head of state to address the highly controversial arena of family life and to challenge the Islamist movement, which opposed any amendment to the existing laws. But the legislation he authored did not endure; on procedural grounds fundamentalists succeeded in overturning the laws after his death.

Under the rubric of an "authoritarian-privatizing" state, Sadat liberalized and modernized the country while forging a new "social contract" with the elites.[1] Retaining for himself dictatorial powers and exclusive control over foreign policy, he offered the upper classes expanded economic opportunities and limited domestic political freedoms. He created the conditions for the bourgeoisie's increased prosperity and influence, crafted a policy of controlled pluralization of political life, and allowed expanded interest-group activity. In particular, Sadat permitted parliament more independent authority, sanctioning the body as a forum for the articulation of middle-class interests. Sadat's measures led to a rise in both secular and Islamic political activity, activity that he expected to remain within the bounds established by the regime.

While Sadat created a multiparty structure, he never intended to preside over a truly functioning parliamentary democracy. The government's ruling National Democratic Party dominated the political system, and although the People's Assembly incorporated diverse political parties, it functioned essentially as a consultative body for the president. In parliament members articulated different voices and distinct opinions, but in reality much of the body protected and endorsed Sadat's authoritarian powers. Although the president allowed controlled pluralism to return to Egypt, at the same time, the regime deliberately demobilized the masses in a conscious effort to prevent any challenge to Sadat's rule.[2] At no time were people from the more humble social classes encouraged to participate in the political process. Civil society, essential to the functioning of democracy and advantageous to national development, was restricted.

Sadat's regime was characterized by a bifurcated economy in which a relatively prosperous private sector coexisted alongside an inefficient and unmanageable public one. A small class of privileged entrepreneurs and rich businessmen at the upper echelons of society became conspicuously affluent while at the opposite extreme the popular classes suffered continued economic decline. As a result of infitah, Egypt's indebtedness increased and fiscal breakdown threatened, so that by the mid-1970s it had become clear that the regime was no longer able to pay back its creditors or borrow money for short-term purposes. Having few alternatives, Sadat invited the International Monetary Fund (IMF) to intervene. In Egypt, just as in all the countries the IMF serviced, the agency promoted its policy of "structural adjustment," which encouraged the privatization of the economy and a reduction in state subsidies on essential goods such as flour, sugar, rice, and gas. The IMF mandated that Sadat allow the market to prevail. While the fund's intention was to reduce government expenditures and streamline the bureaucracy, its policies backfired. In 1977 Egyptians poured out into the streets of Cairo in the largest riots seen in many decades. Sadat's opposition coalesced and nearly toppled his presidency.

In a highly unusual turnaround, based on the West's predisposition toward Sadat and its evolving friendship with Egypt, the IMF allowed Sadat to restore government subsidies on basic products. The international organization capitulated to an agitated and disgruntled urban population bent on influencing social and economic policies. Order was restored, Sadat's regime was rescued, and the president learned the importance of satisfying his poor urban constituency. From this time forward, there was an obvious contradiction in the ideological posture Sadat espoused. While defending Nasirist social welfare policies, he professed commitment to dismantling the socialist economic system of his predecessor. Husni Mubarak, Sadat's successor, has duplicated this balancing act ever since.

Structural adjustment strategies struck women particularly hard. The state reduced its commitment to the welfare economy and trimmed social programs in health and education. Women, who were heavily dependent on the state for employment and services, found fewer opportunities in the paid labor force and faced a truncated social welfare network.

The Social Transformation of Egypt

After consolidating power in 1971 Anwar Sadat began liberalizing the economy and opening up the political system. As Roger Owen has argued, Sadat introduced multiparty politics, from the top down, as a means of finding partners for the regime in a self-styled "liberal" project. In exchange for limited participation in a system of electoral and representative government deliberately designed to disempower the workers and peasants whom Nasir had elevated, middle- and upper-class Egyptians became regime advocates. Not surprisingly, they expected to benefit personally from the policy of infitah.[3]

As Sadat reduced state-sponsored economic activity, he encouraged private investment from local, regional, and international financiers. Economic liberalization was accompanied by a fusion of political and ideological interests between the state and secular forces, but it also co-incided with a state alliance with the widening Islamist groups that also wanted to undermine the Nasirist and leftist forces in the country. Government leaders and Islamic activists shared a common interest in eliminating pro-Nasir support located in universities, professional and trade union associations, and within secular and middle-class circles.[4] The government and its new allies watched over the activities of union-ized workers, syndicated journalists, and university students because of their anticipated aversion to the planned changes in the economic and political arenas.

While undermining the socialist framework built up by Nasir, Sadat sought support for his policies through the construction of a new coali-tion of Islamists, state officials, and middle-class political allies. In par-ticular, since the fundamentalists were looking for a way to reemerge into society after years of repression under Nasir, joining forces with the administration was an expedient way to gain favor with the new regime and also acquire a measure of legitimacy that would authorize them to operate openly.

The alliance between the fundamentalists and the government had serious implications for secular democrats and for women. Gender is-sues became especially contentious because along with Islamist ac-tivism came a renewed social conservatism. One immediate conse-quence was the redrafting of the constitution and a deterioration in women's statutory equality guaranteed during the Nasir years.

The 1971 constitution redefined the meaning of citizenship by stip-ulating that gender equality apply only when it did not contradict the rules of Sharia law. This was a major setback for women and opened the door for a frontal assault on women's right to work and participate in politics and public life as in conflict with the literal readings of Is-lamic texts.[5] In effect, the constitution gave government officials, pri-vate sector employers, husbands and fathers the opportunity to dis-lodge women from their previous gains in the public arena, defending their actions on the basis of religious law. Women, who were now working in the formal and informal economies, saw their livelihoods threatened and their fragile independence curtailed by Islamists who opposed women's presence in the workplace and in the political arena.

Islamists exhorted women to return to their rightful place in the home at the same time that improved female education and inadequate

family resources drove women into the paid workforce. With fundamentalism on the rise, women's independence and their citizenship
rights, never deeply rooted in Egyptian society, once again became subjects of intense controversy. Yet, despite religious campaigns to seclude
women at home and to bar them from the paid labor force, between
1971 and 1981 the high cost of living and reliance on dual incomes
caused the percentage of women in the labor force to actually double
from 7 percent to 14 percent, and this figure did not include women
working in the informal sector in domestic production.[6]

In a friendly gesture toward the Islamists, Sadat amended the constitution once again in 1976 to make Islam the principal source of law-
making; this proclamation empowered the conservative religious
forces even more. Exercising this newly found authority, Islamists in-
voked religious doctrine to chip away at the progress women had
achieved in the previous few decades and in particular used the Sharia
to mobilize the citizenry against laws that defended women's right to
work, receive an education, and participate in public life.[7]

Sadat was trying delicately to maneuver along two contradictory
courses: he compromised with the religious right to offset leftist agita-
tion and at the same time tried to appear progressive at home and to
his allies in the West. To assuage modernizing feminists in Egypt and
to recognize the United Nations Decade for Women in 1975, the government established the Egyptian Women's Organization and the National Commission for Women to handle family planning issues, female illiteracy problems, and child welfare concerns. In addition,
Sadat allowed women to form their own organizations. The Journalists' Union formed a women's committee in 1979; the Progressive
Union Party set up the Federation for Progressive Women in 1982; the
Arab Lawyers' Federation created the Permanent Committee on the
Conditions of Women in 1984; the Arab Women's Solidarity Association came into being in 1984.[8]

During the 1970s Jihan Sadat, wife of the president, emerged as a
self-proclaimed (though by no means universally accepted) spokesper-
son for women's rights in Egypt. Operating in the tradition of Huda
Shaarawi and the early feminists, Jihan Sadat supported charitable activities and reached out to Arabs, Europeans, and Americans to finance
social service projects in Egypt. Following her lead and with the consent of the state, bourgeois Egyptian women created welfare organiza-

tions offering services and income-generating activities to the poor.[9] Jihan's campaign to collect private donations for children and the indigent dovetailed with the government's intention to reduce state spending for social welfare purposes and had the effect of absolving the state of its obligation to its most needy citizens. State leaders had by this time admitted the weak condition of the economy and had endorsed laissez-faire policies. Jihan Sadat's work helped create an ideological and political climate in which the government could abandon costly social undertakings whose only beneficiaries were the poor people Sadat had earlier decided to disempower.

Jihan Sadat was a high-profile first lady who played an important role in her husband's administration. As Earl Sullivan writes,

> Mrs. Sadat had influence and was not shy about using it, especially on behalf of women. Her public life was an ongoing declaration that women were entitled to become educated, to work outside the home, and to have and express political opinions. If she could do it, others could too.[10]

Jihan Sadat was not, however, without detractors. She was publicly accused of mismanaging the social service projects she championed and criticized for her egotism. She was identified with Western consumerism and disliked by many. She was a tireless champion of women's rights, but the controversy that always surrounded her weakened the impact of her ideas. For example, Jihan Sadat wanted to show by example that Egyptian women were capable of earning advanced degrees. To demonstrate this, she had her master's thesis defense, at the American University of Cairo, televised nationally. While her intention might have been honorable, her strategy flopped. Egyptians considered the show an illustration of the excesses of the Sadat regime and an entirely unnecessary indulgence of Jihan's inflated ego.[11] Jihan's unpopularity heightened, popular skepticism toward the regime intensified, and common Egyptians associated the women's movement with the government—even though the two were fundamentally separate. Because Jihan Sadat focused her attention on women's rights, independent feminists became inaccurately identified with the regime. The regime lost support among the people and the women's movement suffered as a result.

Despite their political alliances with the president, religious conservatives excoriated Sadat's wife, condemning her campaign for women's rights as Western-oriented and un-Islamic. The Islamist press discredited Jihan and other women's rights advocates. Fundamentalists jeered at women in the streets and pestered them on public transportation. Through their actions and their ideology, they were building the case for cultural authenticity and female domestication.

After the mid-1970s Islamists grew diverse organizationally and still more aggressive. Their popularity spread at a time when the regime was becoming more detached from the people; it is no wonder that the two groups became adversaries. When Shaykh al-Dahabi, the minister for religious endowments, was assassinated by self-proclaimed militant Islamists in July 1977, the government broke with the religious movement.

By this time Sadat had already drawn close to the United States and Israel, and in keeping with his growing international reputation as a Westernizing modernizer, he wanted to be linked with progressive forces in his own country. To accomplish this end, Sadat announced support for expanded women's rights in the later 1970s. Persuaded by his wife, the president inserted gender quotas into politics to increase women's participation in parliament and level the political playing field. Sadat's liberal move fostered an increased interest in parliamentary politics.

Until the presidential decree on June 20, 1979, which added thirty seats for women in parliament and specified that 10 to 20 percent of the seats in the twenty-six government councils around the country be assigned to women, female representation had been low. In 1957 the first two women entered parliament; between 1964–68 there were eight women members; in 1969 the number had fallen to two. By means of Sadat's decree in 1979 the number of female legislators in the People's Assembly automatically jumped to thirty out of a total of 390 elected officials.[12] In these elections over two hundred female candidates ran for thirty places.[13] Sadat's quota system had an immediately positive impact.

Since he worried about opposition from the right, Sadat assured passage of this law in parliament by employing executive decree. In resorting to an authoritarian procedure, he exacerbated his own isolation and raised controversy over his ruling style. The new legislation did not produce the effect Sadat expected. Theoretically, feminists endorsed this reform because it positively increased the number of women active in public life, which was long overdue. Practically, the progressive community rejected his authoritarian style and did not support him. Sadat was personally attacked by the very constituents whose endorsement he expected and the reform measure was discredited.[14]

After initiating a debate about women's status in society and their rights within the family, Sadat unilaterally reformed the personal status laws in Egypt by invoking executive privilege in parliament. Known colloquially as Jihan's law because of the support lent to it by the president's wife, Sadat's legislation focused on divorce and child custody. By tackling the Islamic personal status codes, Sadat moved far beyond his predecessors—including Nasir, who advanced women's life in the economic and political sectors—by taking on the issue of women's subjugation in the family. Feminists since the turn of the century called for modifications in personal status, understanding that the family harbored the most insidious inequality. Women, they argued, needed to win freedoms at home in order to legitimize their public service. The importance of Sadat's initiative should not be minimized.

Criminal, financial, and commercial laws were covered by civil codes, but family law continued to be governed by the Sharia, and it had been a half century since the personal status law had been updated. Egyptian feminists and women's rights advocates since the early 1900s favored changes in family law and identified polygyny, divorce, and child custody laws as flagrantly adverse to women. They wanted to change women's legal position as well as tackle the cultural biases that hobbled them. Sadat took on an initiative that was certain to provoke the fundamentalists, whose most ardent campaign was to trim women's rights. While Sadat's intention was sincere, his style once again rankled many.

The National Assembly ratified the president's emergency decree in the form of law no. 44, which stipulated that

1. The husband must register his divorce before witnesses at a Registrar's Office and his wife must be officially and immediately informed. Failure on his part to inform her makes him liable to a penalty. A wife has the right to sue for divorce if she disapproves of the marriage and feels "harmed."

2. The divorced wife is entitled to an alimony equivalent to one year's maintenance plus a compensation equivalent to two year's maintenance, and this amount could be increased by the court.

3. The husband who divorces his wife must guarantee her a home if she has custody of his children. He must either find them a home or move out himself.

4. As for custody, the divorced wife automatically gains custody of her children under the age of ten for boys and twelve for girls, subject to extensions by a court decision to fifteen for boys and until marriage for girls.

5. Concerning *bayt al-taah* (house of obedience), confirming an earlier administrative order, a husband can not get the police to return his wife to him by force. The court sanctions the termination of the marriage if the wife refuses to return to the husband.

6. A father must pay child support until his daughters are of marriage age and sons reach fifteen or complete their education.

7. Women's right to work outside the home was confirmed and women were guaranteed equal salaries to men based on comparable levels of education.[15]

Although the new law did not outlaw polygyny or end the male privilege of automatic divorce, it did improve women's rights in the family. However, because the measure was enacted through a counterproductive administrative top-down approach, it would not stand the test of time. Three years after the law was codified, during Husni Mubarak's presidency, its constitutionality was challenged and the case referred to the Higher Constitutional Court. By that time the lower courts, which were often controlled by Islamic fundamentalists, had already ceased enforcing the provisions with any consistency.[16]

Revision of the personal status law sparked controversy and passionate debate between women's organizations, feminist activists, and conservative Islamists. In sermons, newspaper articles, books, and on radio and television programs, Muslim groups pronounced their views on the "appropriate" place of women in Egyptian society. In the popular media and in new organizations created to support women's rights, activist women resisted Islamic conservatism. In particular, women at this time formed the Committee for the Defense of the Rights of Women and the Family, a lobbying group poised to defend previously won gains.

Initially, the committee united diverse groups of women and provided them a single forum from which to advocate their position. Family planning advocate Aziza Hussein and her associates joined the writer Nawal al-Saadawi and her followers to organize against the reinstatement of the statutes of the 1920s. But cooperation was short-lived. In May 1985 Aziza Hussein withdrew from the committee on the advise of Dr. Amal Uthman, minister of social affairs, who counseled Hussein to work behind the scenes and not to engage in open combat.[17] Uthman, the highest ranking woman in government, was used by the regime to undermine feminist activity and to split the coalition apart. She convinced Hussein that if the organization continued to pressure the government officials would invoke the Law of Association, whose intent was to silence oppositional political forces. She warned that since the government interpreted women's advocacy for the personal status law as adversarial behavior women could be arrested and imprisoned. In essence, the government utilized the antidemocratic legal code to intimidate and divide feminist activists.

Aziza Hussein backed off her public crusade, but Saadawi's group continued to advocate its position. Each organization decided to submit a separate argument to the People's Assembly for discussion, but the legislators reviewed only Hussein's, then dismissing it as unrepresentative of the interests of Egyptian women.

In deference to religious activism the Constitutional Court ruled, in May 1985, that the aforementioned personal status law no. 44 of 1979 was unlawful on procedural grounds. Arguing that personal status was not a matter of national urgency, the court concluded that Sadat acted improperly by invoking emergency presidential powers. The Egyptian Parliament then replaced the 1979 ruling with law no. 100 in July 1985. The Islamists were victorious and took another step in their campaign to domesticate women under the strict control of husbands.

The court's ruling was based on standard legal principles concerning the procedure used to pass the law. The judiciary did not address the law's contents. In contrast, because the Islamic movement focused squarely on the substance of the ruling, it brought the essence of the discussion back to the law's content. Supported by most ruling and oppositional religious and political experts, the new law reflected the spirit and the requirements of the Islamic movement.

The new law included important revisions. It stipulated that in the case of a polygynous union the first wife retained the prerogative to seek divorce, but it was no longer her automatic right. Under the modifications she would have to prove to the courts that her husband's second marriage "harmed" her materially and/or mentally and that good mutual relations could not continue. Her right to sue for divorce, previously based on the category of "harm" and resulting from the husband's taking of another wife, would only be valid within the first year of the new marriage. With regard to the couple's apartment, accommodations were now granted to the children during the period of custody and only by extension to their custodian. While the 1979 law awarded lodgings to the wife, the new provision stipulated that once the period of custody ended, the man would be entitled to the return of the house, upon which time the wife was required to leave.

The conditions of alimony also changed, with the husband being responsible for only one year of support. Alimony to the wife would not be paid if the husband divorced the wife for any of the following reasons:

1. the wife disobeyed the husband
2. the wife left the house without the husband's consent
3. the wife worked against her spouse's will
4. the wife's work was seen to jeopardize family life.

The amount of alimony the wife was to receive was determined by a judge, based on his assessment of the husband's financial circumstances. The judge was authorized to enforce new child custody stipulations that returned boys to their father when they reached the age of ten and girls when they turned twelve, although the judge was empowered to grant extensions.

Discussion about the revision of Egypt's personal status law dates back to the nineteenth century, when Islamic reformer Shaykh Muhammad Abduh advocated the restriction of polygyny in an effort to improve women's position in the family. For a century progressive thinkers and activists have echoed Abduh's opinion, and yet only insignificant action has ever been taken to alter the statutes. Even though Huda Shaarawi, Saiza Nabarawi, Duriya Shafiq, Aziza Hussein, and others campaigned tirelessly to empower women in the family, their efforts were largely unsuccessful because family relations remain Egypt's most sensitive and highly contentious social issue.

Even Abd al-Nasir, whose modernizing agenda required the entrance of women into classrooms and workplaces, deliberately kept the state out of people's private lives so as not to alienate religious authorities and undermine his socialist economic planning. When Sadat tackled personal status law, he shattered tradition by situating the state and the judicial system squarely within the domain of the household.[18] Whether Sadat believed it or not, he asserted that the health of the nation depended on the stability of the family and the improvement of women's lives. His government acknowledged women's independent right to work without the consent of husbands, sanctioned equal pay for equal work, and in a controlled way ensured a minimum level of middle-class female representation in parliament.

In the modern Egyptian social system that came into being under Nasir, was endorsed by Sadat, and has continued under President Husni Mubarak, women have entered the educational system in significant numbers and have become part of the paid work force, but they remain subordinate in the family hierarchy. Citizenship combines new public roles for women with culturally traditional concepts of family life. Men are expected to make difficult family decisions and to take responsibility for public policy. Because women are deemed less serious-minded, they are required to obey their husbands and fathers in the family.[19]

The Legacy of Sadat

Anwar Sadat lost control of his country by end of the 1970s. His increasing authoritarianism and personal ostentation alienated the population. Lower- and middle-class workers suffered hardships associated with high inflation, low wages or unemployment, and IMF-imposed structural adjustment policies. Middle-class supporters were uneasy about the Camp David accords, the president's most stunning international victory, and their reviews of his performance were tepid. With his regime teetering and his popularity flat, Sadat clashed with Islamic fundamentalists, whose growing assertiveness further undermined his power.

In retrospect, there were distinct signs revealing Sadat's escalating problems. Uncertain about his authority, Sadat turned to force and repression and renounced what remained of the liberal attributes associated with his regime, in particular political openness and constitutional freedoms. In May 1980 the government promulgated the so-called Law of Shame, a measure whose ostensible purpose was to protect the values of Egyptian society. In reality, the Law of Shame built into the system a new mechanism for punishing opponents. Citizens could be apprehended and incarcerated for repudiating religious, moral, or national values or for publishing material that could offend public sensibilities or undermine the dignity of the state. The government used the law to arrest, try before a special Ethics Court, and convict regime opponents. The edict meted out punishments that included suspension of political rights and economic activity, house arrest, and travel bans; punishments were final and could not be appealed. Shortly after, in September 1981, Sadat ordered the arrests of hundreds of religious extremists, leftists, Nasirists, rightists, New Wafdists, and seemingly anyone else who had ever clashed with the president. The arrests were individually arbitrary and detracted from the government's intended strategy of weakening the Islamic radicals, the president's real opponents.[20]

Women were among those imprisoned. Nawal al-Saadawi, a writer and activist, Safinaz Kazim, a Marxist turned Islamic militant, and Farida al-Naqqash, a member of the opposition party Hizb al-Tagammu' (Progressive Union Party) were taken to al-Qanatir women's prison. About her life as an opponent of the government, al-Naqqash wrote in her memoir, *Prison: Two Tears . . . and a Rose*:

> My husband and I, my children, our family and friends, have had to make a special kind of security for ourselves, to surround our lives with pleasure, affection and psychological fortifications which would incite us against the continued terrorization in all its different forms over these past years. We have been obliged to give our children large doses of political concepts well beyond their years and to fill their lives with the mind and soul of courage and steadfastness. We have shortened their childhood and its pleasures. As contemporary parents we wanted to leave them strong enough to make their own discoveries, not just inherit ours.[21]

The government incarcerated secular feminists and religious fundamentalist women. Their ideologies diverged, but they were viewed similarly as common enemies of the state. International women's groups and global human rights associations staged letter writing and information campaigns to win the release of women prisoners. Most remained in jail for about two months.

The Politics of Reversal Under Husni Mubarak

Following Anwar Sadat's assassination in 1981 Husni Mubarak became head of state. Mubarak was born in the province of Minufiyya in 1928. He graduated from the War College in 1949, rose within the military to become commander of the Air Force, and was appointed vice president in 1975, constitutionally positioning him to assume the presidency in 1981. Mubarak has held onto power since the assassination, and currently is serving his third term (which is to end in 2001). He is supported by most sections of the bourgeoisie, who are dependent upon the regime for jobs and who share the president's ideological conservatism. Like Mubarak's ruling elite, they endorse slow-paced economic reform, preservation of existing class prerogatives, and continuation of a political system that excludes workers and peasants from political participation. Mubarak's ruling party, the largest and most important in the country, is controlled by the president's allies, who are the only candidates allowed to stand for office on the party's list.[22]

Like his predecessor, Mubarak faces challenges from poor and lower-middle-class families who suffer economic hardship and from religious fundamentalists who consider his regime illegitimate. The economic climate in Egypt fuels class antagonisms as debt service payments, inflation, and structural adjustment policies drain resources and cause substantial hardship to the population. While costs for basic necessities continue to climb, wages do not rise commensurately, causing some to assert that unless national wealth is better distributed economic burdens may erode the regime's ability to manage state business and, worse, provoke popular unrest. The Islamists capitalize on economic discontent and preach that only quranic principles can ameliorate conditions of life for the dispossessed.

Islamic activism continues to pose a threat to women's citizenship. Islamists in urban areas carry out a rhetorical campaign glorifying women who stay at home to care for the family. Not only do they celebrate the domestic woman but they excoriate women active in the wage labor force, ignoring the fact that most women work out of plain economic necessity. By popularizing the notion that women are the primary cause of the country's severe unemployment problem, Islamists argue that the only way to increase job opportunities for men is to decrease paid employment for women. As a result, some women have been forced out of their jobs and back into their homes because of the coercive tactics fundamentalists have applied to the government and private sector. Although it is against the law, newspapers have recently begun publishing job advertisements discouraging female applications.[23]

It is axiomatic that questions arise when women become active in the public domain. In the current social and religious climate people ask: What will become of women's work in the family? How will women discharge their duties in the household when they are involved in work outside the home? Will women reduce their commitment to husbands and children? This is an important conversation, but it is also axiomatic that social change is complicated and some dislocation a predictable result. For real change to take place, men's association with the family and their ability to combine politics, work, and home life must also be questioned.

Complex tensions exist under Husni Mubarak's regime. The Islamist movement seeks an indigenous answer to the country's problems and generates considerable sympathy among the people. Worried about the consequences of a provocative opposition, the government has become increasingly dictatorial and abusive of its powers. Competing for attention and also critical of the government is a small, nostalgic, much less well-organized oppositional caucus that demands a democratic alternative to an increasingly absolutist and arbitrary government that uses force and punishment to silence its adversaries. Independent and secular female activists, detached from both movements, are trying to locate a legitimate and lawful space in which to articulate their vision of a modern progressive society.

The system of legislative quotas introduced by Sadat in 1979 was reversed by Mubarak in 1986 and replaced with a new law guaranteeing a seat in each geographic constituency to independent candidates without regard to gender. The 1979 law was controversial from the outset and a subject of contention. Its advocates argued in favor of the quota system because it advanced women's rights by guaranteeing

increased success at the polls. This was considered particularly important in a society in which women were otherwise significantly underrepresented in the political mainstream. Especially in the 1970s and
1980s when conservative attitudes were on the rise, this law was valued as an antidote to growing religious fundamentalism. Through electoral support women had been presented a practical mechanism with
which to confront the repository of laws and traditions that continued
to hobble them.[24] It was also consistent with the International Convention for the Elimination of all Forms of Discrimination Against
Women, which Egypt ratified. The convention endorsed the idea that
in societies experiencing a transitional stage of development special
measures designed to raise the status of women were acceptable until
full equality was achieved.

Mona Qurashi, a journalist for the *Al-Ahram Weekly* newspaper, reported that the government's decision to withdraw women's quotas
generated little protest because the measure won few advocates inside
the administration and even independent women's organizations raised
only muted opposition to its repeal. The most public response came in
the form of a newspaper article signed by women who argued that the
quota system was needed to redress the historic social problems that denied women electoral representation and to mitigate conventional attitudes restricting women's political advancement. As an underprivileged
sector of the society, they argued, women required legal support to ensure their interests and allow their voices to be heard. But their arguments were ignored and the legislation overturned.

By ending the quota system the regime accomplished two goals simultaneously: it built bridges with moderate Islamist groups who were
prepared to join the system as a parliamentary opposition and it disen-
gaged from the controversial feminist policies associated with Anwar
Sadat and his wife, Jihan. Claiming that women were capable of challenging men in their own right, Mubarak justified overturning the law.
But the electoral results did not match the regime's assessment. Whereas, in the 1984 elections, women held 33 out of 448 seats in the People's Assembly, in 1987 the number was reduced to 18, with 14 elected
and 4 appointed. By 1990 there were only 10 women in the Assembly;
7 were elected in their own right and 3 were appointed.[25]

While Egyptian women can exercise political rights through voting,
standing for election, or joining government-approved associations,

the ruling elite has consistently discouraged the establishment of independent political organizations and favored instead the formation of charitable or social groupings. Especially sensitive to feminist action because of the Islamic opposition, Mubarak prefers philanthropic to political activity for women. Yet, like his predecessor, Mubarak finds himself boxed into an irreconcilable contradiction. His regime wants to cast an image to the outside world as progressive and reformist and believes that modernizing women help give the impression that Egypt has a maturing social structure. But Mubarak's government prevents women (and men) from organizing independently. As a result, women have been relegated to the sidelines of important discussions and deliberately shut out of the political mainstream.

In retrospect, the quota system imposed by Sadat failed to produce legislators whose mission was to improve women's rights or generate interest in the women's movement. Mona Qurashi attributes this to three main problems: the nature of the electoral law, which favors the ruling party and effectively stifles political pluralism, the lack of independence exhibited by the women elected, and the conservative religious and social milieu that has dominated Egypt since the 1980s and has invited political and ideological conformity. Yet women's participation in the parliamentary process has occasionally achieved broad-based results for the society. Female parliamentarians, representing a rare unified voice in 1981, succeeded in reversing a government decision that would have paid wage bonuses to the *husbands* of female state employees—not to the workers themselves. Championing the cause of women's independence, the legislators convinced the president to nullify the recommendation submitted by the finance minister.

As a rule, however, female parliamentarians have not often acted as a bloc. Having not yet reached a critical mass in terms of numbers, they have not wielded influence as a group. Typically, they work as individuals or in coalition with their male colleagues to effect changes in the law. In the 1975–76 session, for example, Nawal Amer was among a group of legislators who supported a bill enabling widows to receive the full benefit of their husbands' pensions as well as their own when they retire. While she did not draft this initiative, her support benefited women across the country. Like Nawal Amer, Olfat Kamel and Faida Kamel have represented some of the poorest districts of Cairo. Together with their male counterparts, they secured funding for

schools, mosques, housing units and hospital care for their constituents. Dr. Farkhounda Hassan, with her colleagues, convinced the
government to create an environmental authority to deal with environmental quality and pollution problems.[26]

In the 1950s and 1960s independent activist women viewed the
Nasirist state as a sponsor of women's rights. By the 1980s they
viewed the political leadership as an opponent. In response, some
chose alternative strategies for organization and activity, such as the
Daughters of the Land, a nongovernmental organization created in
1985 in the lower Egyptian town of Mansura to sponsor cultural activities. Women also began meeting casually in study groups and formally in organizations such as the Arab Women's Solidarity Association (AWSA) which came into being in 1984 to encourage women's
fuller participation in the political, social, economic, and cultural life
of the country. AWSA offered critiques of Egyptian and Arab society,
demanded an end to gender discrimination in both the public and private spheres, and called for democracy.[27] Two important events
marked the first year of AWSA's life: the Nairobi International Conference on Women, to which the organization sent a delegation, and
the revocation of the 1979 Personal Status Law, about which the
group had strong views. The conference was inspiring to all who attended, but the real battleground was in Egypt itself, where civil and
Islamic law hindered women's progress. AWSA's spokespeople linked
the personal status law to the wider subject of women's place in Egyptian society and clashed ideologically with Islamic fundamentalists
who opposed AWSA institutionally and criticized its members personally. During the next few years the organization held regular sem-
inars, sponsored an international conference centered in Cairo, and
founded a journal, *Nun*.

The articles in *Nun* spanned many topics: family life, marriage, female circumcision, polygyny, work, poverty, Palestine, Algeria, the
Quran, and fashion. Fundamentalist critics called the articles anti-Is-
lamic and contemptuous of the Sharia; the editors disagreed.[28] For a
few years the group exhibited a high profile, publicly chastising religious leaders or state officials who were disdainful of women's rights.
By 1990 the government had tolerated enough of the group's strident
newspaper campaign and forced *Nun* to stop publication. In the following year it required AWSA to discontinue its activity, dredging up

the 1964 Law of Associations, which prohibited groups from speaking
out on issues related to religion and politics. AWSA was reprimanded,
in particular, for publicly opposing the government's anti-Iraqi position in the Gulf War.

Activist women used the mainstream press to raise public awareness
of women's plight in contemporary culture. Journalists focused,
among other things, on the exploitation of poor women and (minor)
girls who were being married to affluent men from Arab oil-producing
countries through paid business agents. Typically, the girls' fathers acquiesced in the arrangement, were paid a small sum of money, and became vendors in the transaction. Because of the large number of underage girls being "sold" into marriage, the government has now
stipulated that a foreigner must at least be present at the issuing of the
marriage certificate and must certify that the bride agrees to the wedding. The groom must state the date and place of his birth, his religion,
profession, and social standing in the community. He must also indi-
cate his marital status, specifically indicating the number of wives and
children he has in his home country. The newspapers *Nun* and *Al-
Ahram* reported that in 1986 one hundred thousand girls had been
coupled with foreigners through marriage agents.

In this era of Islamism and the politics of reversal, the domestication
of women has become a priority of conservative groups seeking to re-
fashion the moral and cultural order on strict and traditional gender
roles and to glorify the patriarchal family. For Islamists, public society
is synonymous with male culture and citizenship applies to men only.
As large numbers of women accept direction from the religious re-
vivalists and wear the *hijab* (meaning "curtain"), for example, they become invisible to the outside world and shielded from potentially compromising aspects of modernization and development.

Even though upper-class feminists successfully threw off the veil
seventy-five years ago, contemporary women are socialized to accept
traditional dress and the hierarchy of gender that aims to shrink the
arena of public space for women. This has the effect of depriving
women the citizenship rights explicitly guaranteed through constitutional law and international agreements. As the Islamists try to rele-
gate women to the home, their public contributions are ignored.

Islamists are particularly active in the universities, where they typically recruit men and women of rural origin. Fundamentalism also

resonates among members of lower- and middle-class urban society for whom socioeconomic crisis, the nonresponsiveness of the political order, and the weakening of the patriarchal family are realities that threaten the foundation of traditional life. Women who earn an income outside the home diminish the unilateral power of husbands and fathers and introduce new gender relationships into the family. Islamists denounce the changing order, reminding people that women are the standard-bearers of religious and cultural identity. As mothers, women are expected to accommodate a male-defined tradition that obliges them to pass onto the next generation spiritual and national values.[29]

In keeping with the Islamic revival, women have adopted diverse styles of modest dress—sometimes referred to as veiling and other times described as putting on the hijab. The most common form of "wholesome" dress is the headscarf, which covers the hair and neck; sometimes it is worn with a loose robe. The hijab represents more than a piece of clothing; it has become a demarcator of boundaries between men and women, public and private, and even East and West.[30] The phenomenon of modest dressing is complex, and women who don the hijab have diverse explanations for doing so. Modest dress can symbolize a devotion to religion, a commitment to cultural authenticity, a protest against a secular government, a fashion fad, or a means by which a woman can discreetly protect herself while navigating a crowded public space. Large numbers of lower-class women who ride the mass transit system in Cairo as well as middle-class women who work in the government bureaucracy have opted to wear the headscarf.

Arlene MacLeod, who has studied this phenomenon, asks, Is the veil a form of protest, or an accommodation to the patriarchal system? Are women reproducing their own inequality by wearing modest dress, or are they cleverly manipulating the patriarchal conventions in their own interest?[31]

University women of humble rural origin were among the first to "veil." In addition to being unaccustomed to the relatively open environment of the academy, they could not afford an acceptably stylish wardrobe. Wearing a robelike garment over their street clothes allows poor women to save face among their peers. Additionally, by covering, women could create an appropriate space for themselves between skeptical families who were concerned about girls being away from home and radical fundamentalists who criticized women's public status.

Academics observing the recent popularity of the hijab have offered contrasting analyses of the phenomenon. Fadwa al-Guindi asserts that the veil, taken out of context, might be considered backward and in opposition to women's emancipation. When situated within the Islamic setting its meaning changes: women choose the veil to separate themselves from men and as a way to demand respectability in the public domain. For many women the new veiling does serve as protection from public harassment when they go out to work or study. Public space becomes more manageable and better protected.[32]

For Arlene MacLeod the new veil has a double face. It serves as a mediator for women who choose to combine family life with work outside the home and as such protects them against the old-fashioned view that women belong exclusively in the home. Yet accepting modest dress also implies that women need protection when outside the safety of family life. To explain this tension, MacLeod has coined the phrase "accommodating protest."[33]

Mervat Hatem reasons that modest dress was born of economic necessity, the result of declining incomes for middle- and lower-class women who could no longer afford the cost of the commercialized feminine ideal. It was also born of strategic urgency. As the proportion of women working outside the home increased, women appropriated a form of clothing that legitimized their foray into public society.[34] This represented not a choice but a tactic, one that validated women's efforts to moderate a male-dominated and designed culture.

In contrast, Valentine Moghadam suggests that women who don the hijab assent to and confirm men's control over the social and cultural discourse of society. Veiled women allow conservative men to decry women's public role and define their activity as replicating a corrupt Western model. By exalting Islamic dogma, they keep women restrained. Moghadam writes, "What needs to be faced squarely is that Islamic canon law, like any other religious law regulating personal and family life, is inimical to women's emancipation and autonomy."[35]

Fatima Mernissi believes that the reintroduction of the veil represents the desire of the Muslim community to make women disappear. Symbolically, the veil highlights women's illegitimate incursion on male territory.[36] Leila Hessini sees it in a different way, in connection with Moroccan society. Because some women want to retreat from a society that has thwarted their interests, the hijab becomes a shelter, a way in which to withdraw.[37]

Religious women are positively attracted to the Islamic message and accept traditional social views that reinforce the virtues of motherhood and the family. Not only do they embrace the worldview of male Islamists, they enthusiastically espouse it. Islamist men and women accept the need for female education, since educated women produce enlightened children. Even though contemporary research confirms that increased education levels among girls translates into higher rates of paid labor, smaller-sized families, and more active citizens, social conservatives view education exclusively as a tool for raising better children. In Egypt female enrollment rates in primary schools and secondary education have improved dramatically. While 57 percent of the eligible girls were enrolled in primary education in 1970, the number increased to 90 percent by 1990. In 1970 only 23 percent of the entitled girls were enrolled in secondary school, by 1990 the number climbed to 71 percent.[38]

While the Islamists are transmitting their message of religious piety and social conservatism to lower- and middle-class men and women, they are simultaneously reviving society's cultural predisposition against women being active in the public arena. Since only a small number of women hold public office and are not yet in a position as a group to shape public policy, the current discourse around women's issues focuses on the "ideal" woman, who remains at home to care for her family. The Islamic activist Zainab al-Ghazali and the well-known Islamist journalist Safinaz Kazim are among the most visible spokespeople for a redrawing of gender boundaries to restrict women to the home. While Islamist women are forwarding revised categories of female behavior, progressive women are silenced by government decree and hostile legislation. In fact, feminists attribute the revised personal status law of 1985 and the revocation of the reserved parliamentary seats for women as the regime's submission to its fiercest opposition.

In the contemporary climate political and economic activities are becoming increasingly masculinized. By discouraging women from taking jobs in industry and the service sector, the regime accommodates social conservatives who advocate the resegregation of society. The terms of women's citizenship are being eroded as the boundaries within which women can work and engage in public activity shrink.

Women and Work

During the rule of Abd al-Nasir, the state encouraged women to join the paid workforce and assist the nation's economic development. Since that time, severe economic demands on family life have required women to work in the formal and informal labor markets. While long-standing social conservatism and strong predispositions against female employment outside the home have, by necessity, receded in some sectors of society, Islamists continue to criticize women's participation in the public arena. This trend suggests three developments: many Egyptians have become reconciled to the necessity of both private sector employment and government service for women, women's contribution to the family economy is increasingly required, and women must withstand assaults against them by disparaging Islamic militants. For those who accept female employment it is often justified in purely economic terms, thereby legitimizing women's separation from family life.

Paid employment has sometimes paradoxically increased the burdens women face. Women work outside the home and contribute monetarily to the family economy. But there has been little renegotiation of gender roles in the domestic sphere. Almost exclusively, women discharge domestic duties considered consonant with their biological functions.

Women are involved in a variety of economic activities, with the service sector showing the largest concentration, as the following table demonstrates:

WOMEN'S DISTRIBUTION BY ECONOMIC ACTIVITY

ACTIVITY	REGION	URBAN	RURAL
1. Agriculture	2.8	48.8	23.3
2. Mining	0.3	-	0.1
3. Manufacturing	13.4	15.3	14.3
4. Electricity	0.7	-	0.4
5. Construction	1.9	0.3	1.2
6. Trade	14.7	12.7	13.8
7. Transport	4.6	0.1	2.6
8. Finance	3.3	1.2	2.4
9. Government (service)	58.0	21.4	41.7
TOTAL	100.0	100.0	100.0

SOURCE: Za'louf, cited in Daad Mohammed Fouad, *Features of Women's Present Status in Egypt and Their Impact on Development* (Cairo: Cairo Demographic Center, 1994), p. 11.

By virtue of their education and social standing in society, urban upper-class women enjoy a much greater degree of choice in employment. It is not surprising that the higher the level of education, the higher the rates of participation in the paid labor force.[39] Women, however, are subject to the ubiquitous "glass ceiling." While they make up approximately 33 percent of the total number of university graduates, they generally do not reach senior-level positions of employment except occasionally after the age of fifty-five. Hence, women spend the greater part of their working careers in nonleadership roles. In addition, certain fields of work are either entirely closed to women, such as the judiciary (which is controlled by Islamic clerics), or virtually off limits, such as defense.[40] The division of labor by gender reinforces the subordination of women to men in the workplace and also in society in general.

Lower- and middle-class urban women are generally excluded from high-level occupations in the private sector, because they lack business skills and foreign language proficiency, and rejected from prominent public sector jobs because they lack *wasta*, or connections. They find employment, instead, in the expansive government bureaucracy, where wages are low, opportunities few, and challenges virtually nonexistent, or they may be hired as support staff in the private sector. Poor women with few qualifications create their own conditions of employment by working in the informal sector as street vendors, domestics, seamstresses, and the like. Because their labor is not formalized or taxed and does not show up in government figures, informal workers remain "invisible" from a computational point of view. This has the misleading consequence of artificially lowering the number of women reported as working for wages.

Despite growth in the area of paid employment, Egypt still has comparably fewer female workers than other developing societies in the economic south. Valentine Moghadam argues that, unlike Latin America or Southeast Asia, Middle Eastern societies have not successfully moved from the level of import substitution to export-oriented industrialization, the latter being a type of economic development that relies heavily on cheap female labor. As a result, Egyptian women have fewer opportunities for formal employment.[41]

The government has also downsized its bureaucracy to save money. Although Nasir guaranteed holders of intermediate school diplomas and college degrees state jobs, his successors withdrew regime support for this policy, with the result that by 1986 the overall rate of unemployment had doubled from 7.7 percent in 1976 to 14 percent; for men the unemployment figure was 10 percent and for women it was 40.7 percent. These numbers demonstrate the extent to which women are dependent on the state sector for employment. Furthermore, close to half the women who had graduated from college since 1984 and from technical schools since 1983, and who usually seek employment in the public sector, have remained unemployed. Limited employment opportunities frustrate prospective female workers and drive them back into the home, where they are encouraged to accept the conventional role of dependent housewife.[42] As often as not, those who planned to use their education working in the public arena have had their ambitions frustrated.

The situation for women and girls at the state-run textile factory at Helwan offers a glimpse of the worsening conditions of work in one of the public sector's main manufacturing plants. At this shop cost-conscious managers have evaded the country's labor laws by hiring underage girls on a contractual basis. These workers are attractive because they are paid lower wages than permanent employees and receive no pension benefits. Fiscal conservatism has had an effect on mandated day care services at Helwan. While in the past children were regularly given milk, chocolate, and biscuits to eat at the center, they are now offered one biscuit only. Once commonly examined by doctors, children now receive no medical attention. In order to reduce expenses, fewer babysitters are hired to staff the center. Whereas nursing mothers were previously accustomed to one paid hour a day to breast-feed their children, they are now allowed one unpaid hour. As a consequence, many women forgo breast-feeding.[43]

Egypt formally abides by conventions sponsored by the International Labor Organization, and it also ratified the International Convention on the Elimination of All Forms of Discrimination Against Women in 1981. Article 11 of this document stipulates that states shall take all measures to eliminate discrimination against women in the domain of work in order to secure for women: the right to work and to enjoy equality with men; the right to enjoy equal job opportunities; the right to freely choose one's occupation and work; the right of promotion and career security; the right to equal pay, privileges, and treatment for all persons who do the same work, without regard to sex; the right to social security, particularly in retirement, unemployment, sickness, disability and old age; the right to health care, occupational safety and the protection of motherhood and childbearing.

In Egypt labor laws covering both public sector and civil service jobs grant women paid maternity leave for a period of three months, awarded three times during an employee's period of service. Additionally, female employees may take up to two years unpaid maternity leave to care for a child, up to three times during her service. Alternatively, women are allowed to work on a part-time basis for half the salary and sick leaves.

Private sector labor laws protect women against discriminatory behavior and grant women dispensation so that they are shielded from what are considered harmful or compromising activities (working in mines, quarries, bars, casinos, as well as soldering). Women in the private sector also have the right to three fully paid maternity leaves of fifty days each during their period of service. Private establishments with fifty employees must allow women up to one year's unpaid leave to care for an infant, three times during her tenure. The law additionally requires that a business with more than one hundred women workers must establish a nursery program on site.[44]

While social class divisions separate affluent women from their lower-class counterparts, poor women quietly demonstrate impressive organizational and financial skills. In order to manage on limited budgets, they run informal neighborhood co-ops whereby a small number of designated women will go to the market to buy and sell goods for the larger group—thus saving time, energy, and money. Women also operate informal banks. While the operation may vary from group to group, they usually function in the following manner: women from a neighborhood form an association that decides to save a certain amount of money each week or month. The entire sum is then given to each member in turn, based on the particular needs of the members—money needed for burial expenses, a gift, school fees, or a sick family member.[45]

For the last twenty years women have gained valuable labor experience and increased decision-making ability functioning as the sole parent when male family members have gone abroad to work. It is estimated that half the married Egyptian male migrants to Arab countries leave their wives and children behind. As a result, women have singlehandedly raised a generation of children and have asserted themselves in new and challenging ways.[46] They manage their husbands' remittances, deciding how to spend and allocate resources; they take responsibility for livestock and agricultural work in the countryside, tasks which they had not previously performed. Women have even infiltrated into male agricultural or consumer cooperatives, in the interests of discharging family duties. But women's public life in the village continues to be restricted. Females remain largely unwelcome in village councils, political parties, and community associations, and banks and governmental organizations regularly discriminate against them.[47]

As a general matter, women enter the working world, and stay there, to ameliorate the financial hardship their families suffer because of the high cost of living and to achieve upward social mobility. Women participate in the labor market, today, despite criticism from the vociferous and socially conservative Islamist movement, which views the private domain as protected space for women, and, correspondingly, identifies the public domain as belonging exclusively to the world of men. The crowded public transportation system in Cairo is often used as an example of the risks women face when they are in close contact with men.

In one well publicized case a young woman was riding a bus jammed with commuters returning from work. Not able to find a seat, she stood surrounded by workers. Uncomfortably, she found herself being jostled about and then pressed close to the men around her. Although she tried moving away, she was inhibited by the limited space available to her. Before she realized it, a man had reached up under her dress and digitally raped her, thus robbing her of her virginity, reputation, and marriage prospects. When this case was publicized by the press, Islamists blamed the victim for being in male space on a busy city bus.

Men's use of violence to assert their power and dominance shrinks the bounds of women's citizenship and creates fear, psychological distress, and an aversion to public life. Arlene Macleod argues that a traditionalist gender ideology has reemerged that identifies a woman's place in the home and a woman's role as wife and mother. This ideology emanates from the Islamist movement, which argues in favor of the "authentic" family.[48] As a result, public activism has once again become complicated for women. Despite the political right to vote and be elected to parliamentary office and the civil right to paid employment in the public domain, women find their citizenship compromised by a cultural and religious movement committed to traditional gender roles in Egyptian society.

Macleod's research also indicates that while Egyptian husbands maintain in public that they prefer their wives to stay at home, they concede in private that this has become impractical. Women's contributions to the family economy improve its economic standing and often represent the difference between poverty and a decent lifestyle, or between an aspiring middle-class existence and a more humble one. In contemporary Egypt both men and women desire what have come to be recognized as standard comforts: labor-saving devices, a bigger apartment, and educational tutors for their children. While husbands happily enjoy their spouses' income, they have not yet come to terms with changed gender roles in the family.

Conflicting social roles mystify women. Girls are educated in elementary and secondary schools and, sometimes, in university. A significant number of their peers and older female family members work in offices and factories. Women desire comfortable lifestyles and conveniences for themselves and their children, and they enter the labor market to achieve a higher standard of living. But fundamentalists loudly question the legitimacy of women in public life, prompting Egyptian women to confront an essential conflict, which troubles women across the globe: How can working for wages can be reconciled with domestic responsibilities?[49] In fact, the syndrome of the "dual shift," faced by women around the world, applies to Egyptian women as well.

About half the women aged twenty to twenty-nine are engaged in paid employment in Egypt and face the issue of childcare. Many working mothers leave their children with family members, but the more privileged urban women sometimes send their young to private nursery schools, which are relatively few in number and prohibitively costly for most.[50] Women wrestle with their duties, both personally and practically, and try to influence the direction in which the society is moving. But the principle of equality of opportunity for women and men, generally accepted under Nasir, has retreated under his successors. Illegal and regressive practices such as advertising in newspapers for job openings to be filled only by men and calls for women to return to their homes have become commonplace. Those who articulate the view that women should content themselves with looking after their children overlook the fact that the number of women single-handedly supporting their families is 25–30 percent of the total number of breadwinners.[51]

Education and Health Care

Social conditions have become particularly acute for women in the 1980s and 1990s, when structural adjustment policies, World Bank loans, and state-driven austerity measures have substantially reduced the state's commitment to education and health care. The number of school-age children has grown dramatically during these years. Rather than construct new institutional facilities to accommodate the increase, the government has opted to raise class size and the total number of sessions per day. Unable or unwilling to commit adequate funding to its already overextended public education system, the state masks the problem by allowing class enrollments to reach fifty students in elementary and secondary schools and hundreds in universities. Instead of hiring additional teachers to instruct the children, the state arranges morning, afternoon, and sometimes evening classes. The result, not unexpectedly, has been a noticeable deterioration in the quality of instruction, a rise in the absolute number of illiterates in the population, and a growing gap between female and male education in the countryside. In essence, the system of free public education that Nasir constructed is being dismantled by state officials, who are concentrating on privatization, and by international organizations committed to structural changes in the economy.

A similar trend can be discerned in the field of health care, where the state has severely limited its investment. While the number of doctors and nurses has improved in urban areas, there has been a noticeable decline in physician care in the countryside. Although the state is committed to family planning, it now depends, to a large extent, on international donors such as the World Bank and US AID, with mixed results. More than half the resources international organizations disburse are spent on importing contraceptive devices from the United States—many of which are not even approved for the American marketplace.[52]

In response to prohibitively expensive or inaccessible health care, Islamists have set up their own private clinics, which function parallel to those administered by the state. Not only do religiously inspired clinics dispense medication and treatment, but they also spread the message of Islamic revival to poor and working-class clients. According to some human rights' advocates, the proliferation of privately funded Islamic clinics coincides with the distribution of conservative social welfare advice by medical professionals. Islamic advocacy of female circumcision or the genital mutilation of girls, which involves the cutting or the removal of sexual organs, is the area that gives feminists particular anguish. Female genital mutilation is one of the traditional rituals that introduce girls to womanhood and is usually performed on girls before puberty. It can range from a small cut of the clitoris to its excision, to the removal of all the external female genitalia and a sewing up of the vagina. Like many taboo subjects, female genital mutilation is often undiscussed and even more problematic to eradicate. Family planning activist Aziza Hussein observed, "I had . . . been under the impression that this practice had been discontinued in Egypt by law. . . . Upon investigation, we discovered that we did not have a law—but only administrative measures to prohibit the practice in public hospitals."

When Aziza Hussein gathered information in the 1970s about the prevalence of the practice, she discovered that 80 percent of the women who sought care at family planning clinics had been circumcised and themselves intended to circumcise their daughters.[53] Mothers not only carry misinformation about the procedure, they pass it onto their children. For instance, girls are taught that female genitals are unhygienic and that if not cut back will grow long. They are told that clitoridectomy safeguards their honor, while at the same time prevents frigidity, lesbianism, and excessive sexual activity. Raised to believe that uncircumcised girls are unmarriageable, they further expect that circumcision improves fertility as well as maternal and infant mortality. In fact, the reverse is true.[54]

Although girls will often experience psychological as well as physical complications from the procedure, they are forced to submit to it and socialized to accept their lot. Often dressed up and decorated with henna at the ritual, the girls sing and dance, eat special foods, and receive gifts of money. While mothers improperly associate circumcision with Islam, it is a pre-Islamic African tradition carried over into Muslim society. It is still practiced in much of Africa and in parts of Asia and the Middle East. In a study conducted by Doctor Mahmud Karim, professor of gynecology at Ayn Shams University, researchers found that 98 percent of all girls in the Egyptian countryside and poor girls in Cairo had been circumcised (both Muslims and Coptic Christians), while upper-class girls in Cairo were subjected to the procedure 30 percent of the time.[55]

In 1979 Aziza Hussein and the Cairo Family Planning Association arranged a seminar on "Bodily Mutilation of Young Females," which was attended by invited guests from the government, the university community, NGOs, the press, the Arab League, UNICEF, the World Health Organization, and the medical and scientific communities. While this effort helped to bring the issue into public view, the practice has not been stopped. On the contrary, despite legal prohibitions now in place, there is reason to believe that the procedure has even been gaining legitimacy as Islamists revive the belief that it is religiously mandated.

CHAPTER FIVE | Middle Eastern Patriarchy

THE TERM *PATRIARCHY* HAS BEEN used in different ways by theorists from a variety of ideological perspectives. So-called radical feminists apply the term to almost any form of male dominance and connect it to the division of labor between the sexes. Marxist feminists use patriarchy as a category to explain behavior not related to race or class. For others patriarchy may refer to the association of the female with the domestic sphere and her exclusion from public life. Middle Eastern patriarchy—defined generally as a structure of power that operates at different levels of society and endorses the primacy of men—is sustained through both law and custom, and it begins with reproduction.

Women give birth and rear children in the privacy of the family and become dependent on men who work and earn the family's income in the public arena. From an early age, girls and boys are taught to accept the social roles allotted to them and to uphold a system that divides society into male and female spheres. Men derive power from their economic activity and their control over all forms of cultural and ideological production. Patriarchal ideology reinforces the supremacy of men through the mass media, religious and educational institutions, and political organizations.[1]

In Egypt men not only believe that they are duty-bound to support, protect, and defend women, but women as well have internalized the assumption that men offer them safe haven. Accepting the tradition that they represent the source of family honor, women concede to men the business of defining, assessing, and maintaining honorable behavior.

Honor requires that women behave modestly and under no circumstances bring scandal to the family. It is immodest, for example, for girls to behave energetically in public—to laugh out loud, talk boisterously, interact forwardly with men. Even dating is looked upon with disfavor. Girls are taught early in their lives that disgrace comes to families whose girls and women disobey their fathers, brothers, or husbands.

Fatima Mernissi has written that the concepts of female honor and virginity locate the prestige of a man between the legs of a woman. Men derive their status not as a result of their own activities but rather by directly controlling the movements of women related to them by blood or marriage.[2] Women's chastity is aggressively protected and monitored through segregation of the sexes, veiling, strict parental supervision, early marriages, female circumcision, and rigid sex-role socialization. These restraints reinforce the separation of the public from the private sphere and restrict women's activities to the household.[3] Women's collective self-image and their associated status have developed over the centuries, the result of accumulated knowledge, shared experiences, popular rituals, and social interaction. To the extent that women have accepted the place men have allotted them in society, they have been complicitous in creating and recreating the very system of patriarchy that oppresses them.

Especially in the more humble social classes, girls are taught from a tender age that staining a family's reputation shames its male members, jeopardizes a girl's marriageability, and leads, in some cases, to the penalty of death. Boys are persistently treated by adults with an outright preference that borders on adoration. Coddled as babies, admired as youths, heeded as men, their socialization occurs in a permissive environment. Brought up with the certainty that they will be in charge of the private domain, men are taught to control the public arena and any females associated with it.

In Egyptian society the family overshadows the individual, and both men and women fit themselves into the family collective. Marriage is deemed essential for social solidarity, and few provisions are made for single people. Parents sanction the early marriage of their daughters (age varies according to class, geography, circumstance), because marriage provides an important control on female sexuality and freedom. In Egyptian culture social organization is centered on a strong patriarchal family where every woman belongs to "a house," a lineage. Before marriage a girl belongs to her father's house, after marriage, to her husband's. In this way a woman is defined in relation to a man, as his daughter, wife, mother, sister.[4]

When a young Egyptian woman marries, she enters the conjugal household as a dispossessed individual who can best win respect by producing male offspring. Deniz Kandiyoti asserts that patrilineage not only appropriates women's labor and their progeny in the household but also renders women's work and contribution to production invisible. Men take for granted tasks associated with the home and the reproduction of family life, and consider income-generating jobs women hold as subordinate to their own. Women's role in agriculture and in the informal sector are rarely quantified in government statistics or acknowledged by economists, and money earned is often collected by male relatives. Women's stature in the family grows, however, as women age, and reaches a plateau when their sons marry and deliver daughters-in-law for them to dominate. This maintains the circular pattern of subjugation and control in which women actively participate.

Egyptian social scientist Sana al-Khuli recently completed a comparative study in urban Alexandria and rural Beni Suif in southern Egypt on women's attitudes to marriage and the family. In both communities female respondents not only considered marriage a necessity in a woman's life but also had strong ideas about women's place in the home. Conditioned to believe that women must obey their husbands and fathers, women considered this behavior normal and desirable. Furthermore, while 40 percent of the 250 women interviewed by al-Khuli in Alexandria believed that men are better, stronger, and smarter than women, the number jumps to 91.2 percent in rural Beni Suif, a more conservative and traditional community. In the countryside men are viewed by women and by themselves as the main breadwinners who have earned the responsibility to make important social and family decisions. Women admit low self-esteem resulting from their menial social status, a status informed by limited respect from husbands, family members, and society. In the countryside the sexual division of labor is rigid; domestic work is the exclusive duty of women, and salaried jobs are reserved for men.

Whereas rural women appear most heavily dependent on men, al-Khuli found that urban women have become more independent of their spouses, coming to understand that the limits set for them are socially, not biologically, bound.[5] But gender divisions also exist in cities. Though women receive an education and expect to work outside the home for at least part of their lives, they express dissatisfaction with jobs, low wages, domestic responsibilities, and inadequate and crowded transportation systems that inhibit their movements. Because they feel entitled to public space, either working, walking in the streets, riding public transportation, or participating in cultural events, they believe that women can be equal to men if given appropriate training.[6]

In recent years male protection and the economic security women once took for granted when men were the sole wage earners have become increasingly uncertain as unemployment has risen and financial hardships intensified. As the number of female heads of households has swelled, women have taken on more responsibility than ever. This has not, however, structurally altered the relationship between the sexes, suggesting that men fail to comprehend, or even acknowledge, the demands women face in the marketplace and at home.

Whether women overcome the traditional hegemonic social ideas and practices, as socioeconomic changes alter the structure of their lives, will depend upon how successfully they break down the public/private dichotomy, assert themselves in customarily male arenas, and withstand the assaults of conservative and religious forces. Deniz Kandiyoti has coined the term *patriarchal bargain* as a way of understanding the strategies women use to deal with male dominance. The patriarchal bargain varies over time and changes according to class and ethnicity and is useful in explaining the extent to which women either accept the gender ideology imposed upon them or oppose it and generate forms of resistance in its place.[7]

Women's Citizenship Rights in Egypt

Writers Stuart Hall and David Held have argued that citizenship rights are, in essence, entitlements to individuals, individuals whose status as "free and equal" members of society should guarantee them social and public privileges.[8] Yet citizenship models have been built around gender-specific qualities that have deliberately excluded women. As a result, citizenship is not a gender-neutral category but rather a classification reflecting and validating social relations in the family, cultural practices in society, and the sexual division of labor in the workplace. Citizenship rights govern economic activities, political affiliations, legal claims, and family status. Over the course of the twentieth century citizenship rights for Egyptian women have reflected the economic and ideological interests of the regime in power. Throughout very different political regimes prevailing gender ideologies served state power, reinforced religious doctrine, and strengthened the patriarchal paradigm.[9] Remaining constant during these changing times has been the cultural conservatism that permeates social life in Egypt.

During the liberal era, when Egyptians fought for independence from British rule, women's participation in the national movement was welcomed. Indeed, it became a woman's national duty to support liberation efforts. However, once the liberal state consolidated its authority, it did not incorporate women into the ranks of citizen: women were denied the vote and any official public role outside nationalist demonstrations, parades, or strikes. Women were kept at home where their self-validation depended exclusively on their performance as mothers and wives.

A small number of upper-class female activists worked to improve women's status in this period by establishing voluntary social service organizations. They called for the improvement of women's lives through expanded health and educational services and argued that female literacy, salaried employment opportunities, and entry into public life were broad benefits to a modernizing society. Some went further and called for permanent legal revision of the personal status laws that restricted women in the family.

The early feminist movement that emerged during these years sought to link nationalist sentiment with the advancement of women's lives and to guarantee upper-class women new rights in the public arena. Feminist ideas were informed by Islam, cultural authenticity, and national pride, perspectives that remained dominant until the military officers came to power. While activists tried to influence the social and political discourse, the liberal regime's political elite was generally unmoved by their arguments. With no powerful secular or religious constituency committed to redefining gender roles, women's citizenship was rendered only marginally meaningful. Men dominated public life and controlled women in the family.

During Nasir's regime women across social classes began to move out of gender separation. They sent their daughters to school and left their homes to work in textile factories and in offices, as street vendors and professionals. In 1956 women gained the vote and the ability to take part in national life. Their right to enter and influence the public domain was of more than symbolic importance: it allowed women to advance legislation serving women's interests, help frame the national discussion, and persuade colleagues to support their positions. Virginia Sapiro's statement about political participation rings true for Egypt. She writes, "Participation in the governance of one's community is participation in the governance of oneself. Those who are governed but do not govern are not citizens but subjects."[10] When women were granted the vote and the right to engage in political life, they were transformed into citizens with the ability to effect change. They participated in political movements and social organizations, and slowly, in small numbers, entered electoral politics, trade unions, and cultural life, though they remained noticeably underrepresented at the highest levels of the Nasirist state. By entering the public arena, women weakened the boundaries disconnecting public and private experience, expanded their citizenship rights, and advanced their own independence. While women made impressive public gains, family relations changed little, and women continued to be responsible for traditional female tasks.

Abd al-Nasir changed the way Egyptians viewed national development as he combined nationalism, secularism, and state control over all aspects of life with a modified gender ideology. By bringing women into the labor force, he validated women's public role and defended the material benefits derived from their participation. Abd al-Nasir expected Egyptian citizens to adjust their philosophy of life to the changes he instituted. He did not use persuasion to promote the merits of social reform—he mandated it. Women's citizenship rights expanded dramatically during this era, but Nasir was not prepared to confront gender relations in the family or challenge men's authority over their wives by reforming the personal status laws. Because traditional values about women remained constant, social relations in the family changed little and a redefinition of gender identities never really took place.

In addition, no independent feminist movement was allowed to operate during the Nasir years, in keeping with the statist tradition of strong centralized power. The women's organizations that did emerge were connected to Nasir's political parties and limited to advancing the president's agenda. None behaved autonomously.

During the Sadat and Mubarak years there has been a determined shift away from Nasir's populism to a more liberal political and economic philosophy. In this period of relative openness independent women's organizations sporadically reemerged and have attempted to influence public life. In contrast to the Nasir years when frank public discussions were prohibited, feminists have become increasingly vocal about the need to revise personal status law and widen women's freedoms to function in public space. Sadat alleviated some of the hardships associated with the personal status laws but the changes he promoted were reversed under Mubarak who, since the late 1980s and early 1990s, has become increasingly restrictive and cynical about alternative ideological perspectives.

Notwithstanding the important advances in education and employment for women, they are subject to contradictory messages concerning their appropriate place in society. While religious fundamentalism challenges the basis of women's modern citizenship and exhorts women to return to the home, increased educational opportunity combined with widespread economic anxiety encourage women to enter the paid labor market.

Women face an especially uncertain future in a regime that has become increasingly oppressive in response to an ailing economy and a militant Islamic fundamentalist opposition. The government has become defensive about the imposition of IMF-sponsored structural adjustment policies caused by the fiscal decline of the 1970s, closer ties with the United States and Israel, and charges of mismanagement and corruption by people from across social classes. Islamic fundamentalists vociferously condemn the regime and its international allies, denounce secular feminism, and disparage activists as un-Islamic, unpatriotic and mere caricatures of Western models. As long as conservative religious leaders continue to attribute societal tensions and social disorder (fitna) to women, Egyptian feminists can hardly expect Islam to produce a doctrine of liberation.

Future Expectations

Excepting the few women who have participated in intellectual discourse as nationalists and feminists or have joined political movements, the vast majority of female Egyptians remain outside the political arena. Like others who feel themselves peripheral to the mainstream structure of power, women are estranged from the goals of politics and cynical about the political elite's intentions. Encouraging women to develop a stake in politics might be a goal the contemporary feminist movement pursues, but it is a goal severely encumbered by Egypt's history of authoritarian central control. Since the beginning of the liberal era legislative bodies have represented the interests of powerful men for whom gender concerns were at best a matter of indifference, and citizenship rights for women have been manipulated to serve regime needs.

Valentine Moghadam argues that the process of development inescapably leads to the weakening of patriarchy and to progressive changes in women's lives through improved education, expanded employment opportunities, and new strategies to organize family life.[11] Cultural transformation will determine whether Moghadam proves correct. When society allows women to develop an identity as individual beings separate from their husbands and children and with an unquestioned right to the public domain, then progress can be realized and cultural conservatism overcome.

Connecting the private to the public domain and working toward reducing cultural biases can help women achieve full citizenship. In Egypt, despite the number of women who work and belong to social and political organizations, cultural resistance by and toward women exercising individual choice remains. Cultural conservatism, reinforced by religious, ideological, and institutional forces, informs people's thinking and inhibits women's advancement. Gender relations will remain uneven until conventional social beliefs are jettisoned and the full meaning of women's citizenship in social, economic, and political life embraced.

In the final analysis, gender roles cannot be altered until men and women understand how social life is organized and why certain activities are valued over others. Indeed, women will not be accepted as full citizens while their exclusive identification is that of wife/mother. If women's family lives restrict their public roles, their citizenship status is diminished and the control they exert over their lives is reduced.

As long as girls and women are molded into essentially private beings with a singular attachment to the family, they will be easy to marginalize and control. In the privacy of the Egyptian family social control of women translates—to different degrees—into genital mutilation, forced marriages, and segregation. Since reasonable people would identify these abuses as human rights violations, it is inconceivable to separate private life from the public domain and expect that women can become equal members of society. Restructuring family life so that men and women are both responsible for domestic and child-rearing tasks, and both respected as productive members of society, requires major long-term cultural transformation. People must be convinced that a democratic family structure is advantageous to themselves and to society.

In order to accomplish social change, gender equality should be connected with the democratization of the family, the workplace, the community, and the state.[12] Women have the best chance to effect change, enter public life, and assume a share of power when democratic culture prevails. Carolyn Heilbrun has defined power as the ability to take one's place in whatever discourse is essential to action and the right to have one's part matter, whether that is in state politics, family life, community action, or the economy.[13] That is the measure of power to which women should aspire.

Democracy does not guarantee gender equality, but it may be a necessary precondition. In democratic society, where rules, laws, and institutions are universalized and citizenship rights guaranteed, women can campaign for the freedom to work, move around inside and outside the family, organize politically, and rewrite laws that have constrained them socially and legally. In the case of Egypt, women have placed important emphasis on personal status laws. If these laws were reformed as part of a new civil code, then the bedrock of the patriarchal family may give way. With such changes gender asymmetry will come increasingly to be viewed as irreconcilable with modern society. For citizenship to be meaningful in Egypt, the politics of exclusion must end and women must be assured the rights and responsibilities inherent in a just and rational society.

NOTES

PREFACE

1. Moghadam, *Gender, Development, and Policy*, p. 8.
2. Ibid., p. 17.
3. Rassam, "Toward a Theoretical Framework," p. 127.
4. Eisenstein, *Contemporary Feminist Thought*, pp. 19–20.
5. For a full discussion see Hatem, "The Enduring Alliance."

1. ENGENDERING CITIZENSHIP

1. Fowlkes, "Feminist Epistemology Is Political Action," pp. 1-4.
2. Marshall, *Class, Citizenship, and Social Development*, pp. 70, 84, 92, 109; Hall and Held, "Citizens and Citizenship," p. 177.
3. Pedersen, "Gender, Welfare, and Citizenship," p. 985.
4. The following books have recently appeared: Ahmed, *Women and Gender in Islam*; Badran, *Feminists, Islam, and Nation*; Baron, *The Women's Awakening in Egypt*; Graham-Brown, *Images of Women*; Kandiyoti, *Women, Islam, and the State*; Keddie and Baron, *Women in Middle Eastern History*; MacLeod, *Accommodating Protest*; Mernissi, *Islam and Democracy*; Tucker, *Arab Women: Old Boundaries, New Frontiers*.
5. Scott, *Gender and the Politics of History*, pp. 15–25.
6. Ibid., p. 33.
7. Moghadam, *Gender, Development, and Policy*, p. 8.
8. See Ruddick, "Maternal Thinking," pp. 342–67; Elshtain, "The Power and Powerlessness of Women," pp. 110–25. For a dissenting opinion, see Dietz, "Citizenship with a Feminist Face."

9. Dietz, "Context Is All," pp. 10–11.
10. Dietz, "Citizenship with a Feminist Face," pp. 31–34.
11. Pateman, "Equality, Difference, Subordination," pp. 18–19.
12. Eisenstein, *Contemporary Feminist Thought*, p. 7.
13. De Beauvoir, *The Second Sex* (New York: Knopf, 1970), p. 249.
14. MacKinnon, "Feminism, Marxism, Method, and the State," pp. 529–33.
15. Accad, *Sexuality and War*, p. 12.
16. Nelson, "Public and Private Politics," pp. 551–63.
17. Scott, *Gender and the Politics of History*, p. 32.
18. West and Blumberg, *Women and Social Protest*, p. 8.
19. MacKinnon, "Feminism, Marxism, Method, and the State," pp. 535–45.
20. Rassam, "Toward a Theoretical Framework," p. 122.
21. Quoted in Mernissi, "Democracy as Moral Disintegration," p. 38.
22. Ibid., p. 39.
23. Mernissi, *Beyond the Veil*, pp. 31–33 and 42–45; Ghoussoub, "Feminism—or the Eternal Masculine," p. 5.
24. Abdel Kader, *Egyptian Women in a Changing Society*, p. 4
25. Baffoun, "Women and Social Change," p. 230.
26. Mernissi, *Beyond the Veil*, p. 18.
27. Mernissi, *Islam and Democracy*, p. 150.
28. Hammami and Rieker, "Feminist Orientalism and Orientalist Marxism," p. 94.
29. Patemen, *The Sexual Contract*, p. 6.
30. Ibid., pp. 58, 101.
31. See Tetreault, "Civil Society in Kuwait."
32. Rosaldo, "The Use and Abuse of Anthropology," p. 397.
33. Pateman, *The Sexual Contract*, pp. 137–40.
34. Ibid., pp. 222, 225.
35. Scott, *Gender and the Politics of History*, p. 43.
36. Pateman, *The Disorder of Women*, p. 50.
37. See, for example, Okin, *Justice, Gender, and the Family.*
38. For a compelling discussion, see Sharabi, *Neopatriarchy.*
39. Eisenstein, "The State, the Patriarchal Family, and Working Mothers," pp. 16, 44.
40. Moghadam, *Modernizing Women*, p. 110.
41. Sharabi, *Neopatriarchy*, pp. 31–32.
42. Moghadam, *Modernizing Women*, pp. 124–28.
43. Jones, "Citizenship in a Woman-Friendly Polity," p. 6.
44. Sapiro, *The Political Integration of Women*, pp. 30–32.
45. Shanley and Pateman, *Feminist Interpretations and Political Theory*, p. 3.
46. MacLeod, *Accommodating Protest*, p. 17.

47. Interview with Aziza Hussein in *Al-Ahram Weekly*, March 17–23, 1994, p. 14.
48. Pateman, *The Disorder of Women*, p. 130.
49. Sharabi, *Neopatriarchy*, p. 34.
50. Pateman, "The Patriarchal Welfare State," p. 30.

2. LIBERALISM, NATIONALISM, AND GENDER

1. Badran, *Feminists, Islam, and Nation*, pp. 5–10.
2. Badran, "Introduction," in Shaarawi, *Harem Years*, pp. 7–12.
3. Most non-Egyptian ethnic minorities fled Egypt in the 1950s when Nasir inaugurated his nationalist economic policies.
4. Baron, *The Women's Awakening in Egypt*, p. 164.
5. Ahmed, "Feminism and Feminist Movements," p. 158.
6. Badran, "Independent Women," pp. 130, 133.
7. Ibid., p. 132.
8. Graham-Brown, *Images of Women*, p. 224.
9. See Botman, *Egypt from Independence to Revolution*.
10. Abdel Kader, *Egyptian Women in a Changing Society*, p. 23.
11. See Pateman, *The Sexual Contract*; and Joseph, "Gender and Civil Society."
12. Pateman, *The Sexual Contract*, p. 94.
13. Pateman provides full discussion in *The Disorder of Women* and "The Patriarchal Welfare State."
14. Pateman, *The Disorder of Women*, p. 4.
15. Sassoon, "Equality and Difference," pp. 99–100.
16. Al-Sayyid, "A Civil Society in Egypt?" p. 230.
17. Al-Khafaji, "Beyond the Ultra-Nationalist State," pp. 34–39.
18. Mernissi, *Islam and Democracy*, p. 48.
19. Mitchell, "Women and Equality," p. 27.
20. See Shanley and Pateman, *Feminist Interpretations and Political Theory*.
21. Pringle and Watson, "Fathers, Brothers, Mates," p. 230.
22. Vogel, "Is Citizenship Gender-Specific?" pp. 62–63.
23. See Botman, *Egypt from Independence to Revolution*.
24. Kandiyoti, "Introduction," in Kandiyoti, *Women, Islam, and the State*, p. 10.
25. Jayawardena, *Feminism and Nationalism*, p. 49.
26. Hijab, *Womanpower*, p. 38.
27. Stowasser, "Women's Issues in Modern Islamic Thought," p. 10.
28. Abdel Kader, *Egyptian Women in a Changing Society*, pp. 29–31.
29. Hijab, *Womanpower*, p. 40.

30. Hatem, "The Enduring Alliance," p. 24.
31. Badran and Cooke, *Opening the Gates*, pp. 220–26.
32. See ibid. for the full text.
33. See Baron, *The Women's Awakening in Egypt*; and Badran, "Competing Agenda," pp. 203, 206.
34. Badran and Cooke, *Opening the Gates*, p. xiv.
35. Baron, *The Women's Awakening in Egypt*, p. 148.
36. Badran, *Feminists, Islam and Nation*, p. 54.
37. Badran and Cooke, *Opening the Gates*, pp. 134–36.
38. Baron, *The Women's Awakening in Egypt*, pp. 183–84.
39. See Badran, *Feminists, Islam, and Nation*, for more information on Nabawiyya Musa.
40. Badran and Cooke, *Opening the Gates*, pp. 257–58 and 263–69.
41. Badran, *Feminists, Islam, and Nation*, p. 44; and Hatem, "Through Each Other's Eyes," p. 39.
42. Graham-Brown, *Images of Women*, pp. 225–26.
43. Ibid., p. 224.
44. Abdel Kader, *Egyptian Women in a Changing Society*, p. 87.
45. Badran, "Origins of Feminism in Egypt," p. 165.
46. Quoted in Graham-Brown, *Images of Women*, p. 227.
47. Badran, "Independent Women," p. 135.
48. Khater and Nelson, "Al-Harakah al-Nissa'iyah," pp. 467–68.
49. Badran and Cooke, *Opening the Gates*, p. 41; consult Badran, *Feminists, Islam and Nation*, and Shaarawi, *Harem Years*, for detailed information on Shaarawi's life.
50. Badran, "Independent Women," p. 135.
51. Abdel Kader, *Egyptian Women in a Changing Society*, pp. 76, 88.
52. Badran and Cooke, *Opening the Gates*, pp. 279–81.
53. Badran, *Feminists, Islam, and Nation*, p. 125.
54. Abdel Kader, *Egyptian Women in a Changing Society*, p. 92.
55. Badran, "Competing Agenda," pp. 209–11.
56. Khater and Nelson, "Al-Haraka al-Nissa'iyah," p. 468.
57. Fluehr-Lobban, *Islamic Society in Practice*, p. 139.
58. Badran, "Independent Women," p. 137.
59. Khater and Nelson, "Al-Harakah al-Nissa'iyah," pp. 470–72; Badran and Cooke, *Opening the Gates*, p. 352; Badran, "Independent Women," pp. 137–38; and Nelson, "The Voices of Doria Shafik."
60. Quoted in Abdel Kader, *Egyptian Women in a Changing Society*, p. 96.
61. Botman, *The Rise of Egyptian Communism*, pp. 22–23.
62. Aflatun, *Mudhakkirat Inji Aflatun*, pp. 13–17.
63. Botman, *The Rise of Egyptian Communism*, p. 24.

64. Ibid., p. 25.
65. Botman, "Oppositional Politics in Egypt," p. 85.
66. Author's personal interview with Soraya Adham, May 20, 1980, Cairo.
67. Author's personal interview with Latifa al-Zayat, February 9, 1980, Cairo.
68. Ibid.
69. Badran, "Competing Agenda," pp. 201–202.
70. Hatem, "The Enduring Alliance," pp. 27–28.
71. Molyneux, State Policies, p. 6.
72. Hatem, "Egypt's Middle Class in Crisis," p. 412.
73. Sharabi, Neopatriarchy, p. 33.

3. WOMEN AND THE STATE DURING THE NASIR YEARS

1. Al-Khafaji, "Beyond the Ultra-Nationalist State," pp. 34–39; and Mernissi, Islam and Democracy, p. 46.
2. Mernissi, Islam and Democracy, pp. 43, 46.
3. Sullivan, Women in Egyptian Public Life, p. 80.
4. Hatem, "Toward the Development of Post-Islamist Discourses," pp. 39–40.
5. Agarwal, "Patriarchy and the 'Modernizing' State," p. 14.
6. Hinnebusch, "The Formation of the Contemporary Egyptian State," p. 189.
7. Kandiyoti, "Introduction," in Kandiyoti, Women, Islam, and the State, p. 13.
8. Hatem, "Privatization and the Demise of State Feminism," p. 42.
9. For a discussion of the vote see Pateman, "Feminist Critiques," p. 293.
10. Abdel Kader, Egyptian Women in a Changing Society, p. 115.
11. Aflatun, Mudhakkirat Inji Aflatun, p. 172.
12. Quoted in Sullivan, Women in Egyptian Public Life, p. 39.
13. Hatem, "The Paradoxes of State Feminism in Egypt," p. 235.
14. Hatem, "Privatization and the Demise of State Feminism," p. 46.
15. Ibid., pp. 45–46.
16. For a fuller discussion, see Hinnebusch, "The Formation of the Contemporary Egyptian State."
17. Hatem, "The Enduring Alliance," p. 28.
18. Hammam, "Women and Industrial Work in Egypt," p. 58.
19. For a discussion of the role of the state, see Pateman, "The Patriarchal Welfare State," p. 18.
20. Ibrahim, "Cairo's Factory Women," p. 294.
21. The Charter, p. 84.

22. Hammam, "Women and Industrial Work in Egypt," pp. 30–31.

23. Levy, *Each In Her Own Way*, pp. 155–81.

24. Author's personal interview with Amina Shafiq, August 10, 1986, Cairo.

25. Hatem, "Toward the Development of Post-Islamist Discourses, pp. 39–40; and Stowasser, "Women's Issues in Modern Islamic Thought," pp. 12–13.

26. Hatem, "Economic and Political Liberation," pp. 233–35.

27. Hatem "Toward the Development of Post-Islamist Discourses," p. 40.

28. See Radhakrishnan, "Nationalism, Gender, and the Narrative of Identity."

29. Chatterjee, "The Nationalist Resolution of the Women's Question," p. 238.

30. For biographical information on Duriya Shafiq see Nelson, "Biography and Women's History."

31. Badran, "Competing Agenda," p. 217.

32. Hatem, "The Paradoxes of State Feminism," pp. 233–36.

33. Badran, "Independent Women," p. 140.

34. Personal interviews with the author, January 5 and January 18, 1980, Cairo, Egypt.

35. Sullivan, *Women in Egyptian Public Life*, pp. 116–17; and al-Ghazali, *Days From My Life*, pp. 100–1.

36. Watson, "The State of Play," p. 6.

37. MacKinnon, "Feminism, Marxism, Method, and the State," pp. 644–45.

38. Ghoussoub, "Feminism—or the Eternal Masculine," pp. 10–11.

39. Hatem, "Economic and Political Liberation," pp. 231–51.

40. Moghadam, *Determinants of Female Labor Force Participation*, pp. 31–32.

41. Hatem, "Privatization and the Demise of State Feminism," pp. 42–43.

42. Pateman, "The Patriarchal Welfare State," pp. 13–19, 29.

43. Rugh, "Women and Work," pp. 276–77.

44. Sabbah, *Woman in the Muslim Unconscious*, p. 16.

45. Agarwal, "Patriarchy and the 'Modernizing' State," p. 14.

46. Pateman, *The Sexual Contract*, pp. 142, 158.

47. Alifa Rifaat, "Bahiyya's Eyes," in Rifaat, *Distant View of a Minaret*, p. 11.

48. Hatem, "Economic and Political Liberation in Egypt," p. 233.

49. Sangari and Vaid, "Recasting Women," p. 18.

4. GENDER ASYMMETRY DURING THE REGIMES OF ANWAR SADAT AND HUSNI MUBARAK

1. Moghadam, *Modernizing Women*, p. 11.

2. Hinnebusch, "The Formation of the Contemporary Egyptian State," p. 195.
3. Owen, "Socio-Economic Change," pp. 183–84.
4. Hatem, "The Paradoxes of State Feminism," p. 232.
5. Ibid., p. 236.
6. Moghadam, *Modernizing Women*, p. 158.
7. Hatem, "Toward the Development of Post-Islamist Discourses," p. 32.
8. Hatem, "Economic and Political Liberation in Egypt," p. 246.
9. Hatem, "The Paradoxes of State Feminism," p. 237.
10. Sullivan, *Women in Egyptian Public Life*, p. 90.
11. Ibid., p. 92.
12. Walther, *Women in Islam*, p. 228.
13. Sullivan, *Women in Egyptian Public Life*, p. 43.
14. Hatem, "Economic and Political Liberation in Egypt," p. 243.
15. Esposito, *Women in Muslim Family Law*, pp. 61–62; and Fouad, *Features of Women's Present Status in Egypt*, pp. 2–4.
16. Sullivan, *Women in Egyptian Public Life*, p. 37.
17. Reynolds, "Discourses of Social Change," p. 33.
18. Ibid., p. 26.
19. Hatem, "Toward the Development of Post-Islamist Discourses," p. 39.
20. Waterbury, *The Egypt of Nasser and Sadat*, pp. 374–75, 384–85.
21. Harlow, *Barred*, p. 136.
22. Owen, "Socio-Economic Change," p. 194.
23. Tadrus, *Taqyim wad al-mar'ah fi misr,* 91, p. 16.
24. Hatem, "Economic and Political Liberation in Egypt," p. 246.
25. Qurashi, "Women's Thorny Road to Political Equality."
26. Sullivan, *Women in Egyptian Public Life*, pp. 61–72.
27. Al-Saadawi, "Introduction," in Toubia, *Women of the Arab World*, p. 2.
28. Al-Saadawi, *Ma'rakah jadidah fi qadiyya al-mar'ah*, pp. 47–55.
29. Moghadam, *Modernizing Women*, pp. 9, 135–48, 426.
30. Kathleen Moore, Public Lecture at the College of the Holy Cross, Worcester, Mass., March 1995.
31. MacLeod, "Hegemonic Relations and Gender Resistance," pp. 541–45.
32. El-Guindi, "Veiling Infitah with Muslim Ethic," pp. 474–76.
33. MacLeod, "Hegemonic Relations and Gender Resistance," pp. 550–54.
34. Hatem, "The Enduring Alliance," p. 33.
35. Moghadam, "Revolution, Islam and Women," p. 440.
36. Mernissi, "Virginity and Patriarchy," p. 189.
37. Hessini, "Wearing the Hijab in Contemporary Morocco," p. 50.
38. *World Development Report, 1993*, p. 294.

39. Fouad, *Features of Women's Present Status in Egypt*, p. 31.
40. *Legal Rights of Egyptian Women*, pp. 13–14.
41. Moghadam, "Introduction and Overview," p. 17.
42. Hatem, "Privatization and the Demise of State Feminism," pp. 48–49.
43. Ibid., p. 50.
44. *Legal Rights of Egyptian Women*, pp. 9–11.
45. Minai, *Women in Islam*, p. 180.
46. Ibrahim, *The New Arab Social Order*, p. 92.
47. Khafagy, "Women and Labor Migration," p. 20.
48. Al-Sayyid, "A Civil Society in Egypt?" p. 239.
49. MacLeod, "Hegemonic Relations and Gender Resistance," pp. 536, 546–48.
50. Fouad, *Features of Women's Present Status in Egypt*, p. 19.
51. *Legal Rights of Egyptian Women*, pp. 14–15.
52. Hatem, "Privatization and the Demise of State Feminism," pp. 53–55.
53. Levy, *Each in Her Own Way*, pp. 175–76.
54. Toubia, *Female Genital Mutilation*, p. 37.
55. Tadrus, *Taqyim wad al-mar'ah fi misr,* 91, p. 75.

5. MIDDLE EASTERN PATRIARCHY

1. Arat, *The Patriarchal Paradox*, p. 18.
2. Mernissi, "Virginity and Patriarchy," p. 183.
3. Loring, "Introduction," in Abu Nasr, Khoury, and Azzam, *Women, Employment and Development*, p. 6.
4. Jansen, *Women Without Men*, p. 1.
5. Al-Khuli, *Al-usrah wa al-mujtama'*, pp. 25–26.
6. Ibid.
7. Kandiyoti, "Islam and Patriarchy," p. 27.
8. Hall and Held, "Citizens and Citizenship," p. 177.
9. For a discussion of the Sudan, see Hale, "The Rise of Islam."
10. Sapiro, *The Political Integration of Women*, p. 7.
11. Moghadam, "Development and Women's Emancipation," pp. 217–18.
12. Jones, "Citizenship in a Woman-Friendly Polity," pp. 5–8.
13. Heilbrun, *Writing a Woman's Life*, p. 18.

SELECTED BIBLIOGRAPHY

Abdel Kader, Soha. *Egyptian Women in a Changing Society, 1899–1987.*
Boulder: Lynne Rienner, 1987.
Abu-Lughod, Lila. *Writing Women's Worlds: Bedouin Stories.* Berkeley and
Los Angeles: University of California Press, 1993.
——*Veiled Sentiments: Honor and Poetry in a Bedouin Society.* Berkeley and
Los Angeles: University of California Press, 1986.
Abu Nasr, Julinda, Nabil F. Khoury, and Henry T. Azzam. *Women, Employ-
ment, and Development in the Arab World.* Berlin: Mouton, 1985.
Accad, Evelyne. "Sexuality and Sexual Politics: Conflicts and Contradictions
for Contemporary Women in the Middle East." In Chandra Talpade
Mohanty, Ann Russo, and Lourdes Torres, eds., *Third World Women
and the Politics of Feminism,* pp. 237–50. Bloomington: Indiana Uni-
versity Press, 1991.
——*Sexuality and War: Literary Masks of the Middle East.* New York:
New York University Press, 1990.
Aflatun, Inji. *Mudhakkirat Inji Aflatun/tahrir wa-taqdim Sa'id Khayyal* (The
memoirs of Inji Aflatun). Kuwait: Dar Su'ad al-Sabah, 1993.
Afshar, Haleh. "Muslim Women and the Burden of Ideology." *Women's
Studies International Forum* 7, no. 4 (1984): 247–50.
Afshar, Haleh., ed. *Women, Development and Survival in the Third World.*
London and New York: Longman, 1991.
——*Women, State, and Ideology: Studies from Africa and Asia.* London:
Macmillan, 1987.
Agarwal, Bina. "Patriarchy and the 'Modernizing' State: An Introduction."
In Bina Agarwal, ed., *Structures of Patriarchy: State, Community and
Household in Modernising Asia,* pp. 1–28. London: Zed, 1988.

Ahmed, Leila. *Women and Gender in Islam.* New Haven: Yale University Press, 1992.

——"Early Feminist Movements in the Middle East: Turkey and Egypt." In Freda Hussain, ed., *Muslim Women,* pp. 111–23. London: Croon Helm, 1984.

——"Feminism and Feminist Movements in the Middle East, a Preliminary Exploration: Turkey, Egypt, Algeria, People's Democratic Republic of Yemen." *Women's Studies International Forum* 5, no. 2 (1982): 153–68.

Alvarez, Sonia. *Engendering Democracy in Brazil: Women's Movements in Transition Politics.* Princeton: Princeton University Press, 1990.

Anderson, J. N. D. "The Role of Personal Statutes in Social Development in Islamic Countries." *Comparative Studies in Society and History* 13, no. 1, (1971): 16–31.

Anderson, Margaret L. *Thinking About Women: Sociological Perspectives on Sex and Gender.* New York: Macmillian, 1988.

Arat, Yesim. *The Patriarchal Paradox: Women Politicians in Turkey.* Cranbury, N.J.: Associated University Presses, 1989.

Badran, Margot. *Feminists, Islam, and Nation: Gender and the Making of Modern Egypt.* Princeton: Princeton University Press, 1994.

——"Gender Activism: Feminists and Islamists in Egypt." In Valentine M. Moghadam, ed., *Identity Politics and Women: Cultural Reassertions and Feminism in International Perspective,* pp. 202–27. Boulder: Westview, 1994.

——"Independent Women: More Than a Century of Feminism in Egypt." In Judith Tucker, ed., *Arab Women: Old Boundaries, New Frontiers,* pp. 129–48. Bloomington: Indiana University Press, 1993.

——"Competing Agenda: Feminists, Islam, and the State in Nineteenth- and Twentieth-Century Egypt." In Deniz Kandiyoti, ed., *Women, Islam, and the State,* pp. 201–36. Philadelphia: Temple University Press, 1991.

——"The Origins of Feminism in Egypt." In Arina Angerman, Geerte Binnema, Annemieke Keunen, Vefie Poels, Jacqueline Zirkzee, eds., *Current Issues in Women's History,* pp. 153–70. London and New York: Routledge, 1989.

——"Islam, Patriarchy, and Feminism in the Middle East." *Trends in History* 4, no. 1 (1985): 59–88.

Badran, Margot and Miriam Cooke, eds. *Opening the Gates: A Century of Arab Feminist Writing.* Bloomington: Indiana University Press, 1990.

Baffoun, Alya. "Women and Social Change in the Muslim Arab World." *Women's Studies International Forum* 5, no. 2 (1982): 227–42.

Barbalet, J. M. *Citizenship: Rights, Struggle, and Class Inequality*. Milton Keynes, U.K.: Open University Press, 1988.

Baron, Beth. *The Women's Awakening in Egypt: Culture, Society, and the Press*. New Haven: Yale University Press, 1994.

——"Unveiling in Early Twentieth-Century Egypt: Practical and Symbolic Considerations." *Middle Eastern Studies* 25, no. 3, (1989): 370–86.

Beck, Lois and Nikki Keddie, eds. *Women in the Muslim World*. Cambridge: Harvard University Press, 1978.

Bock, Gisela and Susan James, eds. *Beyond Equality and Difference: Citizenship, Feminist Politics, and Female Subjectivity*. London and New York: Routledge, 1992.

Bookman, Ann and Sandra Morgen, eds. *Women and the Politics of Empowerment*. Philadelphia: Temple University Press, 1988.

Botman, Selma. *Egypt from Independence to Revolution: 1919–1952*. Syracuse: Syracuse University Press, 1991.

——*The Rise of Egyptian Communism: 1939–1970*. Syracuse: Syracuse University Press, 1988.

——"Oppositional Politics in Egypt: The Communist Movement, 1936–1954." Ph.D. diss., Harvard University, 1984.

Bystydzienski, Jill M., ed. *Women Transforming Politics: Worldwide Strategies for Empowerment*. Bloomington: Indiana University Press, 1992.

The Charter. Cairo: Information Department, 1962.

Chatterjee, Partha. "The Nationalist Resolution of the Women's Question." In Kumkum Sangari and Sudesh Vaid, eds., *Recasting Women: Essays in Colonial History*, pp. 233–53. New Delhi: Kali for Women, 1989.

Cole, Juan. "Feminism, Class and Islam in Turn-of-the-Century Egypt." *International Journal of Middle Eastern Studies* 13, (1981): 397–407.

Communication Group for the Enhancement of the Status of Women in Egypt. *Legal Rights of Egyptian Women in Theory and Practice*. Cairo: Dar al-Kutub, 1992.

Compendium of International Conventions Concerning the Status of Women. Vienna: United Nations, 1988.

Conway, Jill K., Susan C. Bourque, and Joan W. Scott. "Introduction: The Concept of Gender." *Daedalus* 116, no. 4 (1987): xxi–xxix.

Davis, Kathy, Monique Leijenaar, and Jantine Oldersma. *The Gender of Power*. London: Sage, 1991.

Deeb, Bothayna. *Women's Status, Fertility, and Family Planning in Egypt*. Cairo: Cairo Demographic Center, 1993.

Dietz, Mary G. "Context Is All: Feminism and Theories of Citizenship." *Daedalus* 116, no. 4 (1987): 1–24.

——"Citizenship with a Feminist Face: The Problem with Maternal Thinking." *Political Theory* 13, no. 1 (1985): 19–37.

Early, Evelyn A. *Baladi Women of Cairo: Playing with an Egg and a Stone.*
Boulder: Lynne Rienner, 1993.

Eisenstein, Hester. *Contemporary Feminist Thought.* London: George Allen
and Unwin, 1984.

Eisenstein, Zillah. "The State, the Patriarchal Family, and Working Mothers." In Irene Diamond, ed., *Families, Politics, and Public Policy*, pp.
41–58. New York: Longman, 1983.

Elshtain, Jean. "The Power and Powerlessness of Women." In Gisela Bock
and Susan James, eds., *Beyond Equality and Difference: Citizenship,
Feminist Politics, and Female Subjectivity*, pp. 110–25. London and
New York: Routledge, 1992.

——"Antigone's Daughters: Reflections on Female Identity and the State." In
Irene Diamond, ed., *Families, Politics and Public Policy*, pp. 300–11.
New York: Longman, 1983.

——*Public Man, Private Woman: Women in Social and Political Thought.*
Princeton: Princeton University Press, 1981.

Epstein, Cynthia Fuchs. *Deceptive Distinctions: Sex, Gender, and the Social
Order.* New Haven: Yale University Press, 1988.

Esposito, John. *Women in Muslim Family Law.* Syracuse: Syracuse University Press, 1982.

Ferguson, Ann. *Sexual Democracy: Women, Oppression, and Revolution.*
Boulder: Westview, 1991.

Fernea, Elizabeth, ed. *Women and the Family in the Middle East: New Voices of Change.* Austin: University of Texas Press, 1985.

Fluehr-Lobban, Carolyn. *Islamic Society in Practice.* Gainesville: University
Press of Florida, 1994.

——"Toward a Theory of Arab-Muslim Women As Activists in Secular and
Religious Movements." *Arab Studies Quarterly* 15, no. 2 (1993):
87–105.

Fouad, Daad Mohammed. *Features of Women's Present Status in Egypt and
Their Impact on Development.* Cairo: Cairo Demographic Center, 1994.

Fowlkes, Diane L. "Feminist Epistemology Is Political Action." In Maria J.
Falco, ed., *Feminism and Epistemology: Approaches to Research in
Women and Politics*, pp. 1–4. New York and London: Haworth, 1987.

Al-Ghazali, Zeinab. *Days from My Life.* Cairo: Dar al-Shuruq, 1982.

Ghoussoub, Mai. "Feminism—or the Eternal Masculine—in the Arab
World." *New Left Review* 161 (1987): 3–18.

Goodnow, Jacqueline and Carole Pateman. *Women, Social Science, and Public Policy.* London: Allen and Unwin, 1985.

Graham-Brown, Sarah. *Images of Women*. New York: Columbia University Press, 1988.

El-Guindi, Fadwa. "Veiling Infitah with Muslim Ethic: Egypt's Contemporary Islamic Movement." *Social Problems* 28, no. 4 (1981): 465–85.

Guy, Donna J. " 'White Slavery,' Citizenship, and Nationality in Argentina." In Andrew Parker, Mary Russo, Doris Sommer, and Patricia Yeaeger, eds., *Nationalisms and Sexualities*, pp. 201–17. London: Routledge, 1992.

Haddad, Yvonne Y. *Contemporary Islam and the Challenge of History*. Albany: State University of New York Press, 1982.

Hale, Sondra. "The Rise of Islam and Women of the National Islamic Front in Sudan." *Review of African Political Economy* 54 (1992): 27–42.

Hall, Stuart and David Held. "Citizens and Citizenship." In Stuart Hall and Martin Jacques, eds., *New Times: The Changing Face of Politics in the 1990s*, pp. 173–88. New York: Verso, 1990.

Hammam, Mona. "Capitalist Development, Family Division of Labor, and Migration in the Middle East." In Eleanor Leacock and Helen Safa, eds., *Women's Work*, pp. 158–73. New York: Bergin and Garvey, 1986.

——"Women and Industrial Work in Egypt: The Chubra El-Kheima Case." *Arab Studies Quarterly* 2, no. 1 (1980): 50–69.

Hammami, Reza and Martina Rieker. "Feminist Orientalism and Orientalist Marxism." *New Left Review* 170 (1988): 92–106.

Harlow, Barbara. *Barred: Women, Writing, and Political Detention* (Hanover, N.H.: Wesleyan University Press, 1992.

Harik, Iliya and Denis J. Sullivan, eds. *Privatization and Liberalization in the Middle East*. Bloomington: Indiana University Press, 1992.

Hatem, Mervat F. "The Paradoxes of State Feminism in Egypt." In Barbara J. Nelson and Najma Chowdhuri, eds., *Women and Politics Worldwide*, pp. 226–42. New Haven: Yale University Press, 1994.

——"Privatization and the Demise of State Feminism in Egypt." In Pamela Sparr, ed., *Mortgaging Women's Lives: Feminist Critiques of Structural Adjustment*, pp. 40–60. London: Zed, 1994.

——"Toward the Development of Post-Islamist and Post-Nationalist Feminist Discourses in the Middle East." In Judith Tucker, ed., *Arab Women: Old Boundaries, New Frontiers*, pp. 29–48. Bloomington: Indiana University Press, 1993.

——"Economic and Political Liberation in Egypt and the Demise of State Feminism." *International Journal of Middle East Studies* 24 (1992): 231–51.

——"Through Each Other's Eyes: The Impact on the Colonial Encounter of the Images of Egyptian, Levantine-Egyptian, and European Women, 1862–1920." In Nupur Chaudhuri and Margaret Strobel, eds., *Western*

Women and Imperialism: Complicity and Resistance, pp. 35–58. Bloomington: Indiana University Press, 1992.

——"Egypt's Middle Class in Crisis: The Sexual Division of Labor. *Middle East Journal* 42, no. 3 (1988): 407–22.

——"The Enduring Alliance of Nationalism and Patriarchy in Muslim Personal Status Laws: The Case of Modern Egypt." *Feminist Issues* 6, no. 1 (1986): 19–43.

Heilbrun, Carolyn G. *Writing a Woman's Life.* New York: Norton, 1988.

Hessini, Leila. "Wearing the Hijab in Contemporary Morocco: Choice and Identity." In Fatma Muge Gocek and Shiva Balaghi, eds., *Reconstructing Gender in the Middle East: Tradition, Identity, and Power*, pp. 40–56. New York: Columbia University Press, 1994.

Al-Hibri, Azizah. "A Study of Islamic Herstory: Or How Did We Ever Get Into This Mess?" *Women's Studies International Forum* 5, no. 2 (1982): 207–19.

Hijab, Nadia. *Womanpower: The Arab Debate on Women at Work.* Cambridge: Cambridge University Press, 1988.

Hilmi, Muna. *Bahth maydani 'an musharakat al-mar'ah al-misriyyah fi al-anshitah al-thaqafiyya* (Research concerning the participation of Egyptian women in cultural activities). Cairo: Jam'iyya Tadamun al-Mar'ah al-'Arabiyah, 1990.

Hinnebusch, Raymond A. "The Formation of the Contemporary Egyptian State From Nasser and Sadat To Mubarak." In Ibrahim M. Oweiss, ed., *The Political Economy of Contemporary Egypt*, pp. 188–209. (Washington, D.C.: Center for Contemporary Arab Studies, 1990.

Hoffman-Ladd, Valeria J. "Polemics on the Modesty and Segregation of Women in Contemporary Egypt." *International Journal of Middle East Studies* 19, no. 1 (1987): 23–50.

——"An Islamic Activist: Zaynab al-Ghazali." In Elizabeth Fernea, ed., *Women and the Family in the Middle East: New Voices of Change*, pp. 233–54. Austin: University of Texas Press, 1985.

Hoodfar, Homa. "Personal Strategy and Public Participation in Egypt." In Nanneke Redclift and M. Thea Sinclair, eds., *Working Women: International Perspectives on Labor and Gender Ideology*, pp. 104–24. London and New York: Routledge, 1991.

——"Household Budgeting and Financial Management in a Lower-Income Cairo Neighborhood." In Daisy Dwyer and Judith Bruce, eds., *A Home Divided: Women and Income in the Third World*, pp. 120–42. Stanford: Stanford University Press, 1988.

Human Development Report, 1993. United Nations Development Programme. New York: Oxford University Press, 1993.

Hussein, Aziza. "Recent Amendments to Egypt's Personal Status Law." In Elizabeth Fernea, ed., *Women and the Family in the Middle East: New Voices of Change*, pp. 229–32. Austin: University of Texas Press, 1985.

Ibrahim, Barbara Lethem. "Cairo's Factory Women." In Elizabeth Fernea, ed., *Women and the Family in the Middle East: New Voices of Change*, pp. 293–99. Austin: University of Texas Press, 1985.

Ibrahim, Saad Eddin. *The New Arab Social Order: A Study of the Social Impact of Oil Wealth*. Boulder: Westview, 1992.

James, Susan. "The Good-Enough Citizen: Female Citizenship and Independence." In Gisela Bock and Susan James, eds., *Beyond Equality and Difference: Citizenship, Feminist Politic, and Female Subjectivity*, pp. 48–65. London and New York: Routledge, 1992.

Jansen, Willy. *Women Without Men*. Leiden: Brill, 1987.

Jayawardena, Kumari. *Feminism and Nationalism in the Third World*. London: Zed, 1986.

Jones, Kathleen B. "Citizenship in a Woman-Friendly Polity." *Signs: Journal of Women in Culture and Society* 15, no. 4 (1990): 781–812.

Jones, Kathleen B. and Anna G. Jonasdottir. "Introduction: Gender as an Analytic Category in Political Theory." In Kathleen B. Jones and Anna G. Jonasdottir, eds., *The Political Interests of Gender: Developing Theory and Research with a Feminist Face*, pp. 1–10. London: Sage, 1988.

Joseph, Suad. "Gender and Civil Society, An Interview with Suad Joseph." *Middle East Report* 183 (1993): 22–26.

——"Women and Politics in the Middle East." *MERIP* 138 (1986): 3–7.

Junsay, Alma T. and Tim B. Heaton. *Working Women: Comparative Perspectives in Developing Areas*. Westport, Conn.: Greenwood, 1989.

Kamal, Ihsan. "A Jailhouse of My Own." In Mahmoud Manzalaoui, ed., *Arabic Short Stories, 1945–1965*, pp. 304–16. Cairo: American University Press, 1989.

Kandiyoti, Deniz. "Strategies for Feminist Scholarship in the Middle East." Paper presented at the Twenty-seventh Annual Meeting of the Middle East Studies Association, November 1993.

——"Islam and Patriarchy: A Comparative Perspective." In Nikki Keddie and Beth Baron, eds., *Women in Middle Eastern History*, p. 23–42. New Haven: Yale University Press, 1992.

——*Women, Islam, and the State*. Philadelphia: Temple University Press, 1991.

——"Bargaining with Patriarchy." *Gender and Society* 2, no. 3 (1988): 274–89.

Keddie, Nikki and Beth Baron, eds. *Women in Middle Eastern History*. New Haven: Yale University Press, 1992.

Khafagy, Fatma. "Women and Labor Migration: One Village in Egypt."
    Merip Reports 14, no. 5 (1984): 17–21.
Al-Khafaji, Isam. "Beyond the Ultra-Nationalist State." *Middle East Report*,
    187/188 (1994): 34–39.
Khater, Akram and Cynthia Nelson. "Al-Harakah al-Nissa'iyah: The
    Women's Movement and Political Participation in Modern Egypt."
    Women's Studies International Forum 2, no. 5 (1988): 465–83.
Al-Khayyat, Sana. *Honor and Shame: Women in Modern Iraq*. London: Al
    Saqi, 1990.
Al-Khuli, Sana. *Al-usrah wa al-mujtama'* (Family and society). Alexandria:
    Dar al-Ma'rifah al Jami'liyyah, 1992.
Lazreg, Marnia. "Feminism and Difference: The Perils of Writing As a
    Woman on Women in Algeria." *Feminist Studies* 14, no. 1 (1988):
    81–107.
Lerner, Gerda. *The Creation of Feminist Consciousness: From the Middle
    Ages to Eighteen-Seventy*. New York: Oxford University Press, 1993.
Levy, Marion Fennelly. *Each in Her Own Way: Five Women Leaders of the
    Developing World*. Boulder: Lynne Rienner, 1988.
MacKinnon, Catharine A. "Feminism, Marxism, Method, and the State: An
    Agenda for Theory." *Signs: Journal of Women in Culture and Society* 7,
    no. 3 (1982): 515–44.
——"Feminism, Marxism, Method, and the State: Toward Feminist Ju-
    risprudence." *Signs: Journal of Women in Culture and Society* 8, no. 4
    (1983): 635–58.
MacLeod, Arlene Elowe. "Hegemonic Relations and Gender Resistance: The
    New Veiling as Accommodating Protest in Cairo." *Signs: Journal of
    Women in Culture and Society* 17, no. 3 (1992): 533–57.
——*Accommodating Protest: Working Women, the New Veiling, and
    Change in Cairo*. New York: Columbia University Press, 1991.
Mandelbaum, David G. *Women's Seclusion and Men's Honor*. Tucson: Uni-
    versity of Arizona Press, 1988.
Marshall, T. H. *Class, Citizenship, and Social Development*. Garden City,
    N.Y.: Doubleday, 1964.
——"Citizenship and Social Class." In T. H. Marshall, *Sociology at the
    Crossroads and Other Essays*, pp. 67–127. London: Heinemann,
    1963.
Mernissi, Fatima. *Islam and Democracy: Fear of the Modern World*. Trans.
    Mary Jo Lakeland. Reading, Mass.: Addison-Wesley, 1992.
——*The Veil and the Male Elite: A Feminist Interpretation of Women's
    Rights in Islam*. Trans. Mary Jo Lakeland. Reading, Mass.: Addison-
    Wesley, 1991.

——"Democracy as Moral Disintegration: The Contradiction Between Reli-
gious Belief and Citizenship as a Manifestation of the Ahistoricity of the
Arab Identity." In Nahid Toubia, ed., *Women of the Arab World*, pp.
36–44. London: Zed, 1988.
——*Beyond the Veil: Male-Female Dynamics in a Modern Muslim Society.*
Bloomington: Indiana University Press, 1987.
——"Virginity and Patriarchy." *Women's Studies International Forum* 5, no.
2 (1982): 183–91.
Minai, Naila. *Women in Islam: Tradition and Transition in the Middle East.*
New York: Seaview, 1981.
Mies, Maria. *Patriarchy and Accumulation on a World Scale: Women in the
International Division of Labour.* London: Zed, 1986.
Mitchell, Juliet. "Women and Equality." In Anne Phillips, ed., *Feminism and
Equality* pp. 24–43. New York: New York University Press, 1987.
Moghadam, Valentine. "Gender Dynamics of Restructuring in the Semipe-
riphery." In Rae Lesser Blumber, Cathy A. Rakowski, Irene Tinker,
Michael Monteon, eds., *Engendering Wealth and Well-Being: Empower-
ment for Global Change*, pp. 17–37. Boulder: Westview, 1995.
——"Introduction and Overview: Gender Dynamics of Nationalism, Revolu-
tion, and Islamization." In Valentine Moghadam, ed., *Gender and Na-
tional Identity: Women and Politics in Muslim Societies*, pp. 1–17. Lon-
don: Zed, 1994.
——*Modernizing Women: Gender and Social Change in the Middle East.*
Boulder: Lynne Rienner, 1993.
——"Development and Women's Emancipation: Is There a Connection?"
Development and Change 23, no. 3 (1992): 215–55.
——"Revolution, Islam, and Women: Sexual Politics in Iran and
Afghanistan." In Andrew Parker, Mary Russo, Doris Sommer, and Patri-
cia Yeaeger, eds., *Nationalisms and Sexualities*, pp. 424–46. London:
Routledge, 1992.
——*Determinants of Female Labor Force Participation in the Middle East
and North Africa.* Helsinki: WIDER Working Papers, 1990.
——*Gender, Development, and Policy: Toward Equality and Empowerment.*
Helsinki: World Institute for Development Economics Research of the
United Nations University, 1990.
Moghadam, Valentine, ed. *Identity Politics and Women: Cultural Reassertions
and Feminisms in International Perspective.* Boulder: Westview, 1994.
Mohsen, Safia K. "New Images, Old Reflections: Working Middle-Class
Women in Egypt." In Elizabeth Fernea, ed., *Women and the Family in
the Middle East: New Voices of Change*, pp. 56–71. Austin: University
of Texas Press, 1985.

Molyneux, Maxine. *State Policies and the Position of Women Workers in the People's Democratic Republic of Yemen, 1967–1977.* Geneva: International Labour Office, 1982.

Murphy, Caryle. "Pulling Aside the Veil: Women in the Arab World Struggle Against Male Dominance and Religious Taboos." Repr. William Spencer, ed., *Global Studies: The Middle East.* 5th ed. Guilford, Conn.: Dushkin, 1994.

Nelson, Cynthia. "Biography and Women's History: On Interpreting Doria Shafik." In Nikki Keddie and Beth Baron, eds., *Women in Middle Eastern History: Shifting Boundaries in Sex and Gender*, pp. 310–33. New Haven: Yale University Press, 1992.

——"The Voices of Doria Shafik: Feminist Consciousness in Egypt, 1940–1960." *Feminist Issues* 6, no. 2 (1986): 15–31.

——"Public and Private Politics: Women in the Middle Eastern World." *American Ethnologist* 1, no. 3 (1974): 551–63.

Okin, Susan Moller. *Justice, Gender, and the Family.* New York: Basic, 1989.

Owen, Roger. "Socio-Economic Change and Political Mobilization: The Case of Egypt." In Ghassan Salame, ed., *Democracy Without Democrats? The Renewal of Politics in the Muslim World*, pp. 183–99. London and New York: Tauris, 1994.

Pateman, Carole. "Equality, Difference, Subordination: The Politics of Motherhood and Women's Citizenship." In Gisela Bock and Susan James, eds., *Beyond Equality and Difference: Citizenship, Feminist Politic and Female Subjectivity*, pp. 17–33. London and New York: Routledge, 1992.

——*The Disorder of Women: Democracy, Feminism, and Political Theory.* Stanford: Stanford University Press, 1989.

——*The Sexual Contract.* Stanford: Stanford University Press, 1988.

——"The Patriarchal Welfare State: Women and Democracy." Cambridge: Center for European Studies Working Paper series, Harvard University, 1987.

——"Feminist Critiques of the Public/Private Dichotomy." In S. I. Benn and G. F. Gaus, eds., *Public and Private in Social Life*, pp. 281–303. London: Croon Helm, 1983.

Pedersen, Susan. "Gender, Welfare and Citizenship in Britain During the Great War." *American Historical Review* 95, no. 4 (1990): 983–1006.

Peterson, J. E. "The Political Status of Women in the Arab Gulf States." *Middle East Journal* 43, no. 1 (1989): 34–50.

Phillips, Anne. "Introduction." In Anne Phillips, *Feminism and Equality*, pp. 1–23. New York: New York University Press, 1987.

Pietila, Hilkka and Jeanne Vickers. *Making Women Matter: The Role of the United Nations.* London: Zed, 1990.

Pringle, Rosemary and Sophie Watson. "Fathers, Brothers, Mates: The Fraternal State in Australia." In Sophie Watson, ed., *Playing the State: Australian Feminist Interventions*, pp. 229–43. London: Verso, 1990.

Qurashi, Mona. "Women's Thorny Road to Political Equality." *Al-Ahram Weekly*, February 17–23, 1994.

Radhakrishnan, R. "Nationalism, Gender, and the Narrative of Identity." In Andrew Parker, Mary Russo, Doris Sommer, and Patricia Yeaeger, eds., *Nationalisms and Sexualities*, pp. 77–95. London: Routledge, 1992.

Rasheed, Baheega Sidky, Taheya Mohammed Asfahani, and Samia Sidky Mourad. *The Egyptian Feminist Union*. Cairo: Anglo-Egyptian Bookshop, n.d.

Rassam, Amal. "Toward a Theoretical Framework for the Study of Women in the Arab World." In *Social Science Research and Women in the Arab World*, pp. 122–38. London: Pinter, 1984.

Reynolds, Nancy Young. "Discourses of Social Change: An Analysis of the 1985 Personal Status Law Debate in Egypt." B.A. honors thesis, Harvard University, 1989.

Richards, Alan and John Waterbury. *A Political Economy of the Middle East: State, Class, and Economic Development*. Boulder: Westview, 1990.

Rifaat, Alifa. *Distant View of a Minaret*. Trans. Denys Johnson-Davies. London: Quartet, 1983.

Rosaldo, M. Z. "The Use and Abuse of Anthropology: Reflections on Feminism and Cross-cultural Understanding." *Signs: Journal of Women and Culture in Society* 5, no. 3 (1980): 389–417.

Ruddick, Sara. "Maternal Thinking." *Feminist Studies* 6, no. 2, (1980): 342–67.

Rugh, Andrea B. "Women and Work: Strategies and Choices in a Lower-Class Quarter of Cairo." In Elizabeth Fernea, ed., *Women and the Family in the Middle East: New Voices of Change*, pp. 273–88. Austin: University of Texas Press, 1985.

——*Family in Contemporary Egypt*. Syracuse: Syracuse University Press, 1984.

Al-Saadawi, Nawal. *Ma'rakah jadidah fi qadiyya al-mar'ah* (A new battle in the case of women). Cairo: Sina lil-Nasr, 1992.

Sabbah, Fatna A. *Woman in the Muslim Unconscious*. Trans. Mary Jo Lakeland. New York: Pergamon, 1984.

Sadowski, Yahya. "The New Orientalism and the Democracy Debate." *Middle East Report* 183 (1993): 14–21.

Sangari, Kumkum and Sudesh Vaid. "Recasting Women: An Introduction." In Kumkum Sangari and Sudesh Vaid, eds., *Recasting Women: Essays in Colonial History*, pp. 1–26. New Delhi: Kali for Women, 1989.

Sapiro, Virginia. *The Political Integration of Women: Roles, Socialization, and Politics*. Urbana, Chicago, and London: University of Illinois Press, 1983.

Sassoon, Anne Showstack. "Equality and Difference: The Emergence of a New Concept of Citizenship." In David McLellan and Sean Sayers, eds., *Socialism and Democracy*, pp. 87–105. London: Macmillan, 1991.

Al-Sayyid, Mustapha K. "A Civil Society in Egypt?" *Middle East Journal* 47, no. 2 (1993): 228–42.

Scott, Joan Wallach. *Gender and the Politics of History*. New York: Columbia University Press, 1988.

Shaarawi, Huda. *Harem Years: The Memoirs of an Egyptian Feminist, 1879–1924*. Trans. Margot Badran. London: Virago, 1986.

Shanley, Mary Lyndon and Carole Pateman. *Feminist Interpretations and Political Theory*. Cambridge: Polity, 1991.

Sharabi, Hisham. *Neopatriarchy: A Theory of Distorted Change in Arab Society*. New York: Oxford University Press, 1988.

Siim, Birte. "Towards a Feminist Rethinking of the Welfare State." In Kathleen B. Jones and Anna G. Jonasdottir, eds., *The Political Interests of Gender: Developing Theory and Research with a Feminist Face*, pp. 160–86. London: Sage, 1988.

Singerman, Diane. "Where Has All the Power Gone? Women and Politics in Popular Quarters of Cairo." In Fatma Muge Gocek and Shiva Balaghi, eds., *Reconstructing Gender in the Middle East: Tradition, Identity, and Power*, pp. 174–200. New York: Columbia University Press, 1994.

Sparr, Pamela. *Mortgaging Women's Lives: Feminist Critiques of Structural Adjustment*. London: Zed, 1994.

Stiehm, Judith Hicks. *Arms and the Enlisted Woman*. Philadelphia: Temple University Press, 1989.

Stowasser, Barbara Freyer. "Women's Issues in Modern Islamic Thought." In Judith Tucker, ed., *Arab Women: Old Boundaries, New Frontiers*, pp. 3–28. Bloomington: Indiana University Press, 1993.

——"Liberated Equal or Protected Dependent? Contemporary Religious Paradigms on Women's Status in Islam." *Arab Studies Quarterly* 9, no. 3 (1987): 260–83.

——"The Status of Women in Early Islam." In Freda Hussain, ed., *Muslim Women*, pp. 11–43. London: Croom Helm, 1984.

Sullivan, Earl L. *Women in Egyptian Public Life*. Syracuse: Syracuse University Press, 1986.

Tadrus, Marlin. *Taqyim wad al-mar'ah fi misr, 91* (Assessing the situation of women in Egypt, '91). Cairo: Jam'iyat Tadamun al-Mar'ah al-'Arabiyah, 1991.

Taha, Ahmad Muhammad. *Al-mar'ah al-misriyah* (The Egyptian woman). Cairo: Matba'at Dar al-Ta'lif, 1979.

Tetreault, Mary Ann. "Civil Society in Kuwait: Protected Spaces and Women's Rights." *Middle East Journal* 47, no. 2 (1993): 275–91.

Tillion, Germain. *The Republic of Cousins: Women's Oppression in Mediterranean Society.* Trans. Quintin Hoare. London: Al Saqi, 1983.

Toth, James. "Pride, Purdah, or Paychecks: Gender and the Division of Labor in Rural Egypt." *International Journal of Middle East Studies* 23, no. 2 (1991): 213–36.

Toubia, Nahid. *Female Genital Mutilation: A Call for Global Action.* New York: Women, 1993.

——*Women of the Arab World: The Coming Challenge.* London: Zed, 1988.

Tucker, Judith. "The Arab Family in History." In Judith Tucker, ed., *Arab Women: Old Boundaries, New Frontiers*, pp. 195–207. Bloomington: Indiana University Press, 1993.

Turner, Bryan S. "Outline of a Theory of Citizenship." *Sociology* 24, no. 2 (1990): 189–217.

Vogel, Ursula. "Is Citizenship Gender-Specific?" In Ursula Vogel and Michael Moran, eds., *The Frontiers of Citizenship*, pp. 58–85. London: Macmillan, 1991.

Walby, Sylvia. "Is Citizenship Gendered?" *Sociology* 28, no. 2, (1994): 379–95.

——"Theorising Patriarchy." *Sociology* 23, no. 2, (1989): 213–34.

Walther, Wiebke. *Women in Islam.* Princeton: Markus Wiener, 1993.

Ward, Ann, Jeanne Gregory, and Nira Yuval-Davis, eds. *Women and Citizenship in Europe.* London: Trentham, 1992.

Waterbury, John. *The Egypt of Nasser and Sadat: The Political Economy of Two Regimes.* Princeton: Princeton University Press, 1983.

Watson, Sophie. "The State of Play: An Introduction." In Sophie Watson, ed., *Playing the State: Australian Feminist Interventions*, pp. 3–20. London: Verso, 1990.

West, Guida and Rhoda Lois Blumberg, eds. *Women and Social Protest.* New York: Oxford University Press, 1990.

Women and Work in the Arab Republic of Egypt. Cairo: Ministry of Information, State Information Service, Arab Republic of Egypt, n.d.

World Development Report, 1993: Investing in Health. New York: Oxford University Press, 1993.

The World's Women, 1970–1990: Trends and Statistics. New York: United Nations Publication, 1991.

Youssef, Nadia Haggag. *Women and Work in Developing Countries.* Berkeley: Institute of International Studies, 1974.

Yuval-Davis, Nira. "The Citizenship Debate: Women, Ethnic Processes, and the State." *Feminist Review* 2, no. 39 (1991): 58–68.

Zuhur, Sherifa. *Revealing Reveiling: Islamic Gender Ideology in Contemporary Egypt.* Albany: State University of New York Press, 1992.

INDEX

Abbas School, 34
Abduh, Shaykh Muhammad, 30–32, 86
Abd al-Nasir, Gamal: coup, 28; early years of regime, 43, 50–51, 53–54, 56; educational reform, 56–57; economic policies, 58–60, 71; and feminism, 51–53, 65–69; transformation of the state, 69–71, 111–12; and women at work, 72–73
Adham, Enayet, 46
Adham, Soraya, 45–46
Al-Afghani, Jamal al-Din, 30
Aflatun, Inge, 42, 44–45, 46, 68
Allah, Ahmad Khalaf, 63
Amer, Nawal, 92
Amin, Qasim, 30–32, 70
Arab Feminist Union, 39, 41
Arab Women's Solidarity Association, 80, 93–94
Arab Socialist Union, 62–63
Attiya, Rawya, 56

Bahithat al-Badiya, see Malak Hifni Nasif

Bint al-Nil, 42–43, 65–68
Bint al-Nil magazine, 67

Charter for National Action, 60–61
Committee for the Defense of the Rights of Women and the Family, 85
Communist movement, 27, 41, 43–45, 47
Constitution (1923), 22, 27, 37, 43
Constitution (1956), 54–55
Constitution (1971), 79
Constitution (1976), 80

Daughters of the Land, 93
De Beauvoir, Simone, 7

Egyptian Feminist Party, 42
Egyptian Feminist Union, 35, 37–43, 55, 66
Egyptian Women's Organization, 80

Fadl, Safiyya, 46
Faruq (King), 22
Fawwaz, Zainab, 32, 33
Fitna, 10, 113

Fuad (King), 22, 27

Al-Ghazali, Zainab, 41–42, 69, 97

Hassan, Farkhounda, 93
Hussein, Aziza, 17, 61, 85, 86,
    107–8

International Monetary Fund, 77–
    78, 87, 113
International Woman Suffrage
    Alliance Conference, 35, 39

Kamel, Faida, 92
Kamel, Olfat, 92
Kamil, Suad, 46
Kazim, Safinaz, 88, 97

Law of Shame, 88
League of Women Students and
    Graduates from the University
    and Egyptian Institutes, 45–46

Mubarak, Ali Pasha, 30
Mubarak, Husni: early life, 89; and
    electoral quotas, 90–92; and
    Islamists, 90–91; political
    regime, 89–90, 92, 113; and
    working women, 98–104
Musa, Nabawiyya, 35–36, 37
Muslim Brotherhood, 27, 47, 69
Muslim Women's Society, 42, 69

Nabarawi, Saiza, 39–40, 55, 56, 66,
    68, 86
Al-Naqqash, Farida, 88
Al-Nawfal, Hind, 33
Nasif, Malak Hifni, 33–35
National Commission for Women,
    80

National Democratic Party, 77

Personal status laws: during the
    liberal age, 29, 38, 43, 48–49;
    under Mubarak, 97, 111, 113,
    115; during the Nasir era, 52,
    61; and Sadat, 76, 83–87

Qurashi, Mona, 91–92

Rashid, Fatma Nimat, 42, 68
Rifai, Ahmad, 30

Al-Saadawi, Nawal, 85, 88
Sadat, Anwar: and the economy,
    76–79, 87; and electoral quotas,
    76, 82–83; and personal status
    law, 83–87; political system,
    75–77, 82, 87–88, 91–92; rela-
    tionship with Islamic funda-
    mentalists, 79–80, 82, 87
Sadat, Jinan, 80–83, 91
Saniyah School, 21, 34–35
Al-Sayyid, Amina, 66
Shaarawi, Ali, 38
Shaarawi, Huda, 37–39, 49, 55, 86
Shafiq, Amina, 62, 71
Shafiq, Duriya, 42–43, 49, 54, 65–
    68, 86
Shoukry, Amina, 56
Siyufiyah School, 20, 34
Structural adjustment policies, 77–
    78, 87, 89, 104, 113

Al-Tahtawi, Rifaa, 30, 70
Al-Taimuriyya, Aisha Ismat, 32–33

Veiling, 18, 19, 31, 94–97

Wafd, 22, 26–27, 28, 37

Women's Central Committee of the
    Wafd Party, 37, 39
Women's Committee for Popular
    Resistance, 47
Women's suffrage: during the liberal
    age, 25, 37–38, 43, 111; under
    Nasir, 51, 54–55, 66–67, 70–

71, 112; under Sadat and
    Mubarak, 76, 91

Young Egypt, 27

Zaki, Fatma, 45, 46
Al-Zayat, Latifa, 42, 44–47

Made in the USA
San Bernardino, CA
07 January 2014